Narcissistic Mothers & Abuse Recovery: Healing Workbook- How Sons& Daughters Can Recover From Covert Emotional Abuse, Overcome Codependency & Prevent Future Toxic Relationships

TABLE OF CONTENTS

INTRODUCTION

Times are changing and they're changing quickly. An increasingly competitive and media-centric society forces us to do all we can to get all we can and be all that we can be. Some would call this narcissism, and they just might be right. Everything about our society encourages our idealized self-image, defensiveness and insecurity, and still a strange sense of superiority and entitlement. The internet has made us more sensitive to criticism. It's made us grandiose and more vulnerable, more desperate for the attention and admiration of others. Our self-esteem often hinges on this.

If you've read our other books on narcissism in different realms of our life, you'll recognize those as the hallmark traits of narcissism.

And at the same time, that same fast-paced life has affected our family structures. Divorce hovers at record highs in every Western society. The blended family is increasingly common. Stepparenting introduced into modern mainstream families an unstable and often difficult situation to navigate. And these are relationships which are historically fraught with difficulty, close family relations of various sorts; parents, siblings, grandparents, steps.

The collision of a frenzied word and an increasingly unstable network of family relations has resulted in terrifying statistics and facts so cold you won't want to read them yet. It makes clear the increasingly desperate need to respond to these complications with facts, with new and cutting-edge psychological approaches. It's no longer enough to excuse these things, they've become too dangerous, even deadly.

The fact that you're reading this book now indicates it may be a problem in your own life. Perhaps this problem is narcissism, perhaps the family, perhaps you're just not sure. Chances are, it's both. But you'll know soon enough and you'll be more than prepared to deal with it. Further, you'll be able to help others deal with comparable challenges as needs be.

This book presents all the latest information from leading sources. It collects the newest theories, time-tested concepts, proven practices. It cuts through extemporaneous medical terminology to make the concepts clear and easy to understand. It will help you identify the complexities of narcissism and narcissistic personality disorder, preparing you to deal with them when you have to; be that in somebody else's behavior … or your own. You'll see how narcissism works its way into familial (particularly maternal) relationships. You'll come to know concurrent conditions and the full spectrum of therapies and remedies. It will take more than reading on your part, of course. You may reread some chapters, some of these recommendations are long, slow, and steady approaches, not overnight cures. As we'll see, these problems didn't develop overnight and they won't be solved overnight.

But many of them can be solved, and this book is your first, great step. How do I know? I'm not only a proud writer for this leading series of books, but much of this book plumbs my own personal experience. Like no other book I've presented before, this book reaches into the corners of my own history to uproot the treasures of clear, living examples of the mere theories we discuss.

This time, as they say, it's personal. As you can see, I try to toss in just a touch of humor to keep things light, as the subject matter here may get quite dark indeed. You're bound to learn things you've never come across (and some things even members of my own family still don't know). You'll be uniquely positioned to take these unique and invaluable life lessons into your own life, to improve things for yourself and the people you know and love. You'll have instant resources at your fingertips, practices you can put into practice immediately, and lessons that will stick with you always. You've already begun. Now, all you have to do is keep going.

The best course of action in many cases, and it comes up here again and again, is resolve. It begins with the keystones of emotional intelligence; self-awareness and self-regulation. Know what you need and desire, state your position and hold your ground. Make a plan and stick to it. Our books help you do this in all manner of ways. This one will help you get the element of narcissism out of your family if you can, and out of your life if you must. Just one or two of the things you'll find here could literally save your life. Half of them will create changes you couldn't hardly imagine now. But you will be able to, and soon enough. The old saying goes, "There ain't nothin' to it but to do it."

And time is running out. If you've read this far, if you've opened this book at all, a problem has likely been growing for some time. You've likely ignored it, denied it, and eventually had to face the fact that there is a problem. So it could already be worse than you think. These are degenerative conditions, and they sometimes deteriorate with greater rapidity as we get older. Time may already be running out. You've made your plan, now stick to it. This is your ground. Find your position and hold your position.

You're not alone. You're armed with every tool you need to persevere. All you need is this book, your own resolve, and time enough to make it work. You can do it, we can help! Turn the page, and let's get to work.

SECTION 1: NARCISSISM

CHAPTER ONE: Definitions, Types, Symptoms, Coping

What is it?

Narcissism and the condition *narcissistic personality disorder* (NPD) share the same core principles; exaggerated self-importance and a disproportionate need to be admired and paid attention to. They demonstrate a notable lack of empathy, often have troubled relationships, have low self-esteem and are overly sensitive to criticism. Sufferers of NPD, unlike those who are mere narcissists, are unable or unwilling to recognize the destructiveness of their behavior.

Narcissists (and, of course, sufferers of NPD) are often both dissatisfied with and dissatisfying in their personal, professional, and fiscal relationships. Narcissists lack empathy. They have an idealized image of themselves and cannot abide having it violated or challenged. Their disappointment stems from not getting the sufficient, unquestioning support which narcissism generates.

Experts believe that between1% and 6% of adults may suffer from NPD and even more children, parents, children, business partners, coworkers, intimate partners and family members are often directly affected.

We all have a little but of some of the qualities of narcissism. We all want to be supported, we crave positive affirmation. But we don't demand it, and we don't act out if we don't get it.

And we all have some concern for others, some sense of empathy. Narcissists lack this essential human quality; they don't care what effect their behavior has on others.

A lot of people take narcissist as self-love, but that's not quite right. The narcissist actually is racked with low self-esteem. They can only delude themselves about their true nature while they remain enthrall to their idealized self-image.

There are varying degrees of NPD and narcissism.

Types of Narcissism

It's important to know the differences between narcissistic personality disorder and garden variety narcissism. NPD is best marked by:

- Inflated self-importance
- Feeling of superiority
- Deep need for admiration
- Fragile self-esteem
- Resistance to criticism
- No regard for the feelings of others
- Feelings of depression and isolation
- Hidden feelings of inadequacy, shame, humiliation
- Lack of self-confidence

Narcissism is signaled by:

- Exploitation and manipulation
- Feelings of entitlement
- Lack of empathy

- Lack of self-shame
- Lack of self-awareness

NPD can be tough to diagnose because the charm and charisma are central to narcissism and related conditions. The narcissist and NPD sufferer are apt to surround themselves with those who adore them, so they're rarely challenged, and antisocial behaviors are ignored and even encouraged.

The three different types of narcissism are *malignant, grandiose* and *vulnerable.*

Sufferers of grandiose narcissism were probably treated exceptionally in childhood, as if they were better than other children. This contributes to their general feelings of superiority and entitlement. It generates aggressive, dominant behaviors and attitudes. They have an outsized impression of their own importance and they have little regard for the importance of others.

A vulnerable narcissist is often abused and overly criticized in childhood, creating a psyche which is overly sensitive to criticism and harbors feelings of anxiety and inadequacy.

Malignant narcissism, a psychological syndrome, is best described as an extreme mix of aggression, narcissism, sadism, and antisocial behavior. Malignant narcissists are generally grandiose and extroverted. They revel in hostility, dehumanizing people and undermining families and organizations.

A hypothetical diagnostic category which is not listed in the Diagnostic and Statistical Manual of Mental Disorders (DSM-IV-TR), malignant narcissism includes elements of NPD, as well as other personality disorders (paranoid, antisocial and sadistic). Social psychologist Erich Fromm coined the term in the 1960s. He described malignant narcissism as a severe mental illness, and the quintessence of evil and a severe mental illness. It's the inclusion of the sadistic element which results in a sadistic psychopath.

But because it's a hypothetical diagnosis, not everybody agrees. Some believe that true psychopaths have paranoia which the malignant narcissist lacks. The malignant narcissist may be able to admire others, which the psychopath cannot. Malignant narcissists often identify with powerful figures and take their place in a community; psychotics cannot. Cults and terrorist groups and more appealing to the malignant narcissist than to the true psychotic. Sexual, serial, and mass murder investigations often entail malignant narcissism.

Signs and Symptoms of NPD

Narcissism and NPD often present themselves with outsized self-importance, and fantasies of brilliance, success, beauty, or power. Exhibitionism is common. They often rage about themselves and demonstrated indifference to or contempt for others. as they require constant attention and praise. Their behavior often modulates between indifference to others and rage about themselves. They are prone to depression and are given to exploitative and manipulative behaviors with others. They expect preferential treatment from others and rare give the same to others. They often have attachment and dependency issues, though their relationships are often self-serving and superficial. They tend to monopolize conversations, belittle others with whom they disagree or to whom they feel superior. Hence, arrogance, pretense, and boastfulness are common behavioral patterns in those with NPD and narcissism.

Narcissists hate to be criticized and often become impatient or angry, contemptuous, even rageful. They are unable to regulate their behaviors or emotions and often cannot deal well with change or stress. Narcissists often report feeling depressed and moody, harboring feelings of insecurity, shame, vulnerability, and humiliation.

They expect obedience, exceptional treatment, and agreement from others. They are often insulted and feel betrayed by disagreement.

Narcissists and those with NPD commonly face scholastic or professional challenges, depression and anxiety, ill-health, substance abuse, premature death, and suicide. They're generally controlling and distant and opportunistic. They're often bullies, especially when their ego gratification needs are not met.

Narcissism and NPD can be hard to diagnose and to treat. Even finding the root causes can be difficult, but experts agree it goes back to early childhood, where a potential narcissist was treated to too much praise (grandiose narcissism) or too little (vulnerable). Though genetics may also play a hand. A type A personality, generally outgoing, may be prone to grandiose narcissism. A type B personality may react to overly critical treatment in childhood and develop vulnerable narcissism.

Experts also agree that narcissism and NPD develop during the teenage years and early adulthood. It's harder to spot the signs in children, as they lack the self-control to be anything other than narcissistic. Parenting classes, family therapy, and treatment of correlating conditions are good ways to deal with blossoming narcissism in teens.

Narcissists often feel threatened by others who have other gifts or excel, those who are popular and confident. Narcissists are prone to jealousy of and contempt for such people and often exhibit passive-aggressive personality traits (even sometimes the disorder).

The History of NPD

Narcissistic personality disorder was first diagnosed about fifty years ago, though the concept goes all the way to the Ancient Greek myth of Narcissus, who was so taken by his own reflection in a pond that he stayed in its banks until his death. Vanity, arrogance, hubris (unrealistic haughtiness) are common qualities of the narcissist.

Austrian Otto Rank wrote an early piece on narcissism in 1911, revolutionizing the study of narcissism and NPD. Sigmund Freud followed that up in 1914, asserting that narcissism, was connected to the libido, which governs survival instincts. Narcissism results when the libido is turned inward, according to Freud.

It was followed up in 1914 with the publication of *On Narcissism: An Introduction* by

Dr. Sigmund Freud. Freud's notion of narcissism was that it was connected to the libido, which guides survival instincts. If the libido is directed inward, it results in narcissism. Children often exhibited *primary narcissism.*

Freud believed the limited libido energy should be turned outward, establishing relationships and resulting in behaviors such as volunteerism. Freud believed that a healthy, satisfied psyche had a balance of inward and outward libidinal energy.

The 1950s and '60s brought new attention to narcissism and a three-tiered construct including normal adult narcissism, normal infantile narcissism, and pathological narcissism. Grandiose and vulnerable narcissism were designated as the two varieties of narcissism.

Normal adult and infantile narcissism are just that; normal. Adults face challenges (emotional, financial, physical) which require some measure of self-confidence and could and should generate feelings of healthy self-esteem. It helps when avoiding perfectionism and negative self-talk, which can generate depression, self-doubt, and a host of other unhealthy conditions and even disorders.

A little bit of the self-confidence is even more important in children, who cannot avoid perfectionism or self-regulate on their own, as adults can.

Decidedly not normal, pathological narcissism, grandiose and vulnerable was seen as the root of certain behaviors, not all of them criminal. Alexander the Great was a narcissist who thought of himself as a demigod and had no empathy for his weary army.

England's Henry VIII was a narcissist with infamously shallow and self-serving intimate relationships. French emperor Napoleon Bonaparte was a narcissist, racked with insecurity about his height to such an extent that a complex was named for him. One has to imagine he'd be quite pleased with that.

Ancient Rome's Nero was so narcissistic that he burned his how city in order to clear the land for an expanded personal palace. An actor, he forced

Roman citizens to witness his hours-long (and apparently dreadful) performances or be killed trying to escape. His last words are said to have been, "What an artist dies in me."

Self-obsession and lack of empathy helped make Germany's Adolph Hitler the malignant narcissist that he was. From Emperor Nero of Ancient Rome to US President Donald Trump, history is rife with controversial diagnoses of narcissism and NPD. But it's not just about world leaders. Entertainers such as Madonna and Kanye West are famous for their narcissism (and largely only famous because of it).

Contrarily, Winston Churchill, Sir Paul McCartney, and Dolly Parton are well-known for their empathy and altruistic deeds.

Narcissism and Social Media

Narcissism has found new life on social media, where self-promotion is so prevalent, and where insults are so common. People are either selling themselves in one capacity or another, or they're degrading somebody else's efforts to do the same. Algorithms feed you news stories based on your preferences, creating a cyberworld which reflects the user's own idealized self-image. Facebook and Twitter are rife with narcissists, though Facebook offers more opportunities for exhibitionism, which the narcissist craves.

Cyberbullying is a new expression of narcissism, which is closely related to other abuses behaviors (substance, physical, psychological, sexual, identity abuse). Cyberbullying touches on a lot of those, and satisfies the narcissist's need for power and control. Cyberbullying can quickly escalate to one of its concurrent abuses, so take great care with such things.

Roughly five percent of women and about exhibit NPD behaviors enough to warrant a diagnosis. Yet more girls use social media (43%) than boys (31%) up to fifteen years of age. Women post more selfies than men, signaling the focus of exploitation, manipulation, and obsession with self-image which help define a narcissist.

Narcissism and NPD can be hard to diagnose and to treat. Even finding the root causes can be difficult, but experts agree it goes back to early childhood, where a potential narcissist was treated to too much praise (grandiose narcissism) or too little (vulnerable). Though genetics may also play a hand. A type A personality, generally outgoing, may be prone to grandiose narcissism. A type B personality may react to overly critical treatment in childhood and develop vulnerable narcissism.

Experts also agree that narcissism and NPD develop during the teenage years and early adulthood. It's harder to spot the signs in children, as they lack the self-control to be anything other than narcissistic. Parenting classes, family therapy, and treatment of correlating conditions are good ways to deal with blossoming narcissism in teens.

It's a lot to digest, unless you've read one of our other books on narcissism. In that case, now you're nicely refreshed on the subject. If not, you've now got a functioning knowledge of narcissism and narcissistic personality disorder. You'll need that, of course, if you're going to be able to conquer whatever narcissistic parenting situation you might be facing. And things only get a little more complex from here we delve deeper into narcissism, what it can do, and what can be done about it.

CHAPTER TWO:
Variations of Narcissism and How to Deal with Them

Variations of Narcissism

It's probably not surprising that there is more to narcissism than just grandiose, vulnerable, and malignant. There are varying degrees of megalomania, some are more dangerous and antisocial than others. Some narcissists may be prone to substance abuse, others not at all. And the better you can identify the degrees of narcissism, the better equipped you'll be to deal with them.

Covert narcissism, for example, is really a variation on grandiose narcissism, not vulnerable (as you might imagine). Covert narcissism is favored by those who prefer the appearance of humility. It's a more subtle approach, one which is a bit more passive-aggressive than the bragging and exhibitionism so often associated with grandiose narcissism.

Overt narcissism is more along the lines of your classic narcissist, with lots of outward behavior to ensure others' attention. They often have superiority complexes, hero complexes, or even God complexes. These complexes are just as they sound; the hero complex designates the sufferer as key to survival, the superior complex is signaled by feelings of superiority. Other complexes include inferiority, martyr, victim, Napoleon, Don Juan, Oedipus /Electra (impulse to marry the opposite-gender parent).

Sexual narcissists have insecurities and overt or covert behaviors of a sexual nature. They are sometimes sex addicts, and often use sex to manipulate others. They may also lie to their sexual partners, they may withhold sex, or they may insult the other's prowess in the bedroom or their worth as a person outside it. This narcissist may be prone to physical abuses, child abuse, molestation, harassment, and rape.

Unlike the other variations of narcissism, circumstantial narcissism seems to have no connection to childhood or rearing. Genetics don't seem to play a part either. Instead, the circumstantial narcissist may develop as a result of sudden success, as in the case of entertainers and politicians. It's true that these careers generally develop over time and a person only seems to be an overnight sensation. But the circumstantial narcissist is apt to remain humble and grounded during the early, difficult years. It's perhaps a contributing factor to the circumstantial narcissism when it finally strikes.

Passive-aggressive narcissism has different facets of the other types of narcissism; the covert narcissist's desire, the abuses of the grandiose narcissist, the withdrawal of the vulnerable narcissist. They share the manipulative traits all narcissists exhibit.

How to Deal with a Narcissist

Dealing with narcissists and those with NPD requires emotional intelligence, which is based on self-awareness and self-regulation. You have to know your strengths and weaknesses, know your triggers, know how you're like to react to certain, often stressful influences such as the narcissist is likely to present.

It's crucial to remember that narcissists require a second party to manipulate. They need that person to adore them, to give them the supportive attention they need. So the first thing to do with a narcissist is not to play into it. Don't offer them the compliments they're fishing for. Don't fawn. There's little good to be had in challenging them or otherwise critiquing them. That also only feeds the cycle, turning narcissistic feelings into outward behavioral abuses. In fact, the best thing to do with a narcissist is just walk away, though that may not be acceptable. Just walk away from your narcissistic boss when he or she is talking to you won't do your career much good.

Deprioritize the narcissist (just the opposite of what they want). You can do that in little ways; just carry on and ignore the narcissist as much as is possible. Stay neutral, do not begin criticizing a third party along with the narcissist. Just opt out of the whole affair, or say and do as little as possible.

While you're deprioritizing the narcissist, you'll naturally be prioritizing yourself. Dealing with a narcissist can be stressful, it may create anxiety. Self-care may be required, so be mindful of what your needs are and make sure they're seen to. This could be as simple as counting to ten to relieve stress or taking some time alone to clear your thoughts. Mediation may be helpful. Or self-care could entail being ready to declare. Certain behaviors are not acceptable, and you may need to establish that. If your boss is the narcissist, this may be difficult. Always suggest, never demand. The narcissist will refuse your demand in any case.

But be prepared. Narcissists will rob you of your privacy, your recognition, your self-respect, and your resources. You have to protect yourself when dealing with a narcissist.

But you'll need a plan. Narcissists are delusional in a lot of ways, so simply pointing out a truth or two won't do any good. You can set boundaries, and you should, but know what the narcissist will not respect them. So when the inevitably cross the line, you'll have to act. But … how?

Don't argue; it won't help and it will only make things worse. Narcissists will not be moved, they will not be convinced of anything other than their own opinion, which can be the only right opinion. Don't bother going down the rabbit hole with a narcissist.

Think about having a subject in mind, and when things get narcissistic, change the subject to that. Have something ready, something you know will appeal to the narcissist without appealing to the correlating behavioral abuses. New movies are always good, so are sporting events; current events may be a little dicey. But since the narcissist cares for little other than themselves, you're not about to shake up a bee's hive.

Remember not to take any of their behavior personally. And you may be withstanding some verbal and identity abuses in dealing with narcissists, but it's important to keep in mind that their abuses have nothing to do with you. So externalize their behavior from yours, the one has nothing to do with the other. You may even be able to externalize the narcissist's behavior from the narcissist themselves. They weren't always a narcissist, it happened to them beginning from childhood. In this way, it's their fault. They may not yet be able to self-regulate, and they may not even be self-aware enough to realize their behavior needs regulating to begin with.

Don't be fooled. The narcissist may be overt to manipulate you into their service. So not only should you not empower the narcissist with words, don't let them work their way into your brain. They have that capacity, and they often lack the empathy which regulates behavior. Once they're in your head, they're not likely to respect what's already there. They can't afford to. The narcissist has to wipe out whatever reality pre-existed so they can replace them with the deluded self-image which keeps them going.

Don't expect anything from a narcissist. They take, they don't give. You won't get praise, you won't get support, you won't get satisfaction. Narcissists have a transactional world view; one person's advantage must come at somebody else's disadvantage. A compliment for you is an insult to them because they didn't get the compliment. And for the narcissist, the transaction only goes one way; into their personal coffers, not yours.

There's not much benefit to be had in having a relationship with a narcissist. It may give you a new appreciation for the healthy relationships in your life. It may inspire you to go out and create some new friendships with people who are worthy of it and worthy of you. If you can get free of the narcissist (and you probably can) then you probably should.

Narcissists as Abusers

One of the main reasons narcissists are to be avoided at just about all costs is that they're abusers.

And these abuses can be not only dangerous, but deadly. Abusive relationships can be very hard to get out of because abusers are manipulative and can confuse and beguile your intentions.

They're masters of the abuse cycle; friendly, angry, abusive, contrite. The friendliness will only go on as long as the abuser is being treated as they desire (especially the narcissist). Once that ends, the inevitable anger surfaces. That justifies the abuse (in the eyes of the narcissist anyway). After the abuse, contrition is required to restart the cycle. But don't confuse contrition for legitimate shame or guilt; the narcissist doesn't feel those things. The contrition stage of the abuse cycle is particularly easy for the manipulative narcissist.

How to Treat NPD

In this book, we're focusing on narcissism and abuse, so we're not going to hit disorder treatment too hard. But since narcissism can become narcissistic personality disorder, a brief look at disorder treatment here is important.

NPD is largely behavioral, as we've seen. So favored treatments include psychodynamic behavioral (with the focus on unconscious causes) and cognitive behavioral (focus on conscious causes) techniques, as well as psychopharmacological management (prescribes medications).

Mentalization-based therapy may be effective. Mentalization is a disciplined way of considering the desires, beliefs, and emotions which underlay our personal interactions with others. The umbrella term includes social skills and emotional intelligence. We've already written about them in other books, and we've got lots to cover here. So let's move on!

Group therapy is often used to treat narcissism, because narcissism is so interactive and reliant on personal interaction. Antidepressants and antipsychotics may be prescribed in some cases. Generally, prevention is best. Once a person suffers from full-blown narcissistic personality disorder, it can be impossible to reverse.

Leaving a Narcissist

This book, sadly is all about troubled relationships between parents and their children. Those are (or should be) among the closet relationships of our lives. You've no doubt come into this book hoping to save that relationship, and that is what we hope to do. But the sad truth is that these close relationships can sometimes not be saved. One has to be ready to turn their backs on a parent or adult sibling in the name of self-care. The abuses can be serious, perhaps even deadly. The sad story of soul singer Marvin Gaye, shot by his own father, is proof that such things happen, and it's likely that they happen a lot more commonly than you think. Experts estimate that it happens about 500 times a year in the United States and have been doing so for the past thirty years. That's 15,000 murders in the US alone.

And it's not just an American thing either.

Australian John Sharpe was convicted of deliberately shooting his pregnant wife and infant daughter with a speargun. Englishman Ceri Fuller stabbed his three children and then killed himself. Fred and Rose West, of England, were convicted of killing two of their children, an may have killed more.

Physical or Sexual abuse requires one recourse; to physically remove yourself or any children from the interaction. This may require court intervention and the help of experts in the field, including social workers and psychologists.

Psychological abuse isn't the same kind of crime as the other two, though it's just as damaging. Taunting, deferential treatment, verbal abuses; all are common in psychological as well as other types of abuse. Substance abuse is often a catalyst for psychological abuse. What's worse, the offender often doesn't even know that what they're doing is abusive at all. That's what leads them to resist treatment. Psychological abuse is often a central element to child abuse, as we'll soon see.

One bit of good news is that some cycles of abuse can be broken. Made aware of psychological abuse, such an abuser may be able to change his or her behavior. Substance abuse can be treated and managed, if not cured (though this is arguable). It's going to be a long and challenging decision to make.

So if you're trapped in one of these cycles and you've tried everything in order break it. You may just have to cut that person loose, mother or father or sister or brother. This is uniquely important in these cases and here's why. People in your family, parents in particular, may feel that they are uniquely positioned to be forgiven for their abuses. This is common to narcissists, who expect exceptional treatment in any case. But being a family members may realize that they're not likely to get cut off. You've been accepting their behavior all your life, after all. They may simply discard your feelings or their responsibilities as, "You're my brother, it's different," or, "we're family, it's different." But of course it's not different. Nobody has the right to abuse another person. In fact, I would personally offer that family members deserve more respect, not less; certainly not none

So consider drawing the line and letting go. Don't do it on a whim, but don't be willing to let yourself be abused; not by your parents, your siblings, your lovers; not by anyone.

Once again, it's about making a plan and sticking to it. Have strategies prepared to counter their behavior, be prepared for their resistance. A narcissist will not want you to leave them, as you and others are essential tools in their narcissism. They may cling to you, beg you to stay. When that doesn't work, they'll probably become angry, betrayed, and exhibit the precise abusive behaviors which brought you to cut them off in the first place. Or they realize you're of no value to them, that you offer no utility, and just lose interest in you. In that case, be glad; you got off easy.

Be prepared for what they might say and do, but also what you will say and do. You'll want to make a clear case, even knowing that they won't listen. You'll want closure, you'll want to know you were clear and concise and made your needs and desires clearly known. You can't control others, but you can control yourself. Here's where we revisit self-awareness and self-regulation, concepts we'll return to often in this and in our other books too.

While this unfortunate chore should probably be done one-on-one, so the narcissist doesn't feel ganged-up on. That will only fuel their defensiveness and their anger. The narcissist loves to feel like the underdog, that they're being persecuted. But that doesn't mean you can't get a little help preparing (as you're doing right here, right now). Talk to people you may have in common (always in confidence), talk to friends who've had similar situations and relationships (you may know more of them than you realize). Consult experts online. The more you know, the more prepared you'll be and the smoother things may go.

Once you've made your plan and you've declared your position, stand your ground. You cannot back away from your position against an abusive partner of whatever caliber. If you back down, you guarantee a repetition of the cycle of abuse. And once you back down, the abuser will never respect you, they will never take you seriously. It won't be easy, and the abuser will know it. But it's vital that, once you've prepared and decided and acted, you must follow through.

Once you've gotten away, stay away. Stick to the plan, whatever it is! It won't be easy, it never is. It's hard enough to stay away from an ex-lover or childhood pal who may be a bad influence. But cutting yourself off from your mother or father, from abusive adult child or sibling, is sometimes the only sorrowful choice you can make. Does it sound impossible? Maybe that's because of childhood references to the importance and permanence of family. It's engrained in us on every level to value family; picture books instill images of idealized family life, parents instill the notion into their children's heads from an early age (even if they scarcely believe it themselves). We're told to obey, to be respectful. "Do as I say, not as I do."

We grow up thinking we are attached to family, as if we will always be living in the same house. From an early age, it's instilled in us that we can't leave the home, and that's largely correct. But once a person has their independence, that has to be respected by others, whatever their complex or disorder. It's not a matter of lack of respect, but of new self-respect. The rules of your childhood no longer apply, because you are no longer a child. This may be something the abusive family member may have (conveniently) forgotten.

There's another complication to breaking with a family member. You've probably severed ties with intimate partners before, old friends, coworkers or business partners. You have a frame of reference for that. But with family, you likely have no experience in letting them go. If you've known these people your whole life, it may be hard to imagine life without them. But you have to ask yourself if having a relationship with an abuser is really living.

In fact, you've probably already imagined life without them. It will have challenges, but it will also have rewards; self-respect, a sense of worth, a respite from stress and anxiety and maybe even a longer (and certainly happier and healthier) life.

And who knows? You may just shock this abusive family member into recognizing the need for them to change. It will be too late for your relationship, but you may have other siblings who would benefit. Or you could benefit others you don't know or don't know well.

You should consider a total and complete break. I know, it may give you a chill just to consider such a thing. But if you're trapped in abusive relationship which you can't treat, you have to be ready to do whatever you have to do in the name of self-care.

We're focusing here on parents and children and other abusive relationships, however, and marriages can certainly become abusive. In this case, consider a court-appointed go-between during handovers of the children. It's going to be awkward, but it would be safe and it will be civil.

You may grieve after ending the relationship, but don't let that send you back. The good times will be easy to remember. Instead, remember the abuses, the need you felt to get free. Stand your ground, and be prepared to hold that position for the rest of your life.

And as you're mourning, don't imagine that the abuser in mourning you. Most likely a narcissist in this case (because that's the book you bought), the abuser will blame you, vindicate themselves, play the victim and the martyr and these will only reaffirm the narcissist's position.

Infamous Cases

This book focuses on cases of child-parent abuse (in one direction or the other). But this divergence was important to fully understand the full spectrum of disorders, providing context for the subject of narcissistic parental abuses. So, to help illustrate these disorders and complexes into perspective, let's take a look at a few classic and well-known (more infamous than famous) examples.

Actor Charlie Sheen has pleaded guilty to domestic abuse charges. According to sources, charges have been levelled against other famous actors too, including (but not limited to): actors Mel Gibson, Mickey Rourke, Steven Seagal, Sean Penn, as well as singers James Brown, Rick James (who did prison time for his alleged abuses). Johnny Depp has a long and ugly history of abuse charges against former wife, actress Amber Heard. Numerous decisions in courts of law have supported the actress's legal rights.

And it's not just male-on-female abuse either. *Clueless* actress Stacey Dash faced charges of beating and slapping her boyfriend.

Our study of narcissism has taken into even darker corners of social interaction; abuse and abusive relationships. If you're reading this book, odds are good that you're involved in some sort of narcissistic familial relationship, or you know and want to help somebody who does. Our focus, as we state in the title, will be on narcissistic mothers, though every member of a family unit has their part to play, as victim or abuser, depending on the dynamic. Narcissism in families is not just about mothers. In fact, because narcissism is a learned set of traits, it's virtually certain to be a shared problem in any family who is exposed to it. If there's a narcissistic parent, there's likely to be a narcissistic child, for example. They say that we all become our parents, and the flipside is also true; our children become us.

So lets turn our attention to the complex family interrelationships in question and see how narcissism may affect them before moving on to other disorders and complexes and how they too can affect a family.

As we do, I'll be leaning heavily on my own family experiences (as I promised, or forewarned, in the introduction). Just a few reassurances. These stories are true, the names are fake, and most of them are no longer with us.

SECTION 2: THE FAMILY

CHAPTER THREE:
Narcissistic and Abusive Parents

The first think you'll note about narcissism is that it takes basically the same shape and includes the same behavioral hallmarks. The definition of narcissism doesn't change when they're applied to one group or another. True, there are different types as we've seen, but they all share the same basic traits (lack of empathy, lack of self-awareness and self-regulation, idealized self-image, etc). If you don't remember them all off the top of your head, don't worry; we'll review them in context.

What varies is the narcissist; their temperament, their measure of authority, their place in the relationship. A narcissistic boss is a different matter than a narcissistic friend. You can abandon a friendship with relative ease compared to several your connections to your boss, after all. To make matters worse, the more power a narcissist has in your life, and over your life, the more likely they are to be abusive.

And when they're your parents (or adult children) that can be made all the more complicated. Children are trained to obey their parents (though some simply do no, usually due to poor parenting practices). Those formative years are just when abusive parents establish abusive practices and habits which they can use to control their children well into adulthood. And controlling through manipulation is central to the narcissist's success.

A narcissistic parent can be a holy terror to their children. It's all the more terrible that children are exploited this way all of their lives. Parents are the people whom a child is supposed to be able to trust, to rely upon for protection, not to be manipulated by them. But perhaps it shouldn't be surprising. Children lack the mental acumen and experience which their parents have. And when those parents are narcissists, possibly unaware of what they're doing, it's a problem which may never stop.

It's worth noting here that narcissists, unlike those suffering from narcissistic personality disorder, generally do know what they're doing, and may even want to take steps to correct it (though they usually will not do that, at least not on their own).

This is where, as I mentioned, I'll be going into the dark corners of my own life to illuminate our way through this journey. I was raised by narcissists to varying degrees (it was Los Angeles, after all), and they do present excellent (and wholly unique) examples of some of the concepts we'll be looking at here.

So let's take a closer look at the hallmarks of narcissism again, this time with an eye toward its manifestation in and effect on parents and their treatment of their (child or adult) children.

Narcissistic parents generally live through their children, are possessive of them, and engages in marginalizing competition with them. The narcissistic parent often sees the independence of their child, at whatever stage of life, as a threat. This is so because narcissists are radically insecure about being abandoned or losing control, and the child's independence does indeed portend to both of those situations. The narcissist wields unrealistic expectations to keep the child in their shadow. As with most narcissistic relationships, love is conditional, and those conditions are the satisfaction of the narcissist's needs and wants.

It's easy to picture the over-eager stage mother or the so-called *tiger mom*, each pushing their kids to almost impossible heights or achievement. Because for the narcissist, it's all about them. The child is a reflection of them, their success or failure. But this isn't the case with every such dynamic necessarily. In a world where absentee parenting due to double-income households (a widespread economic necessity in the United States), parents have to work harder when they have the chance. A real danger is child neglect, for a boy or girl to grow up without the proper support and guidance. We're not about to come down on parents for urging their children on to excellence.

Parents are correct in seeing their children as reflections of their childrearing skills and strategies (the cause-and-effect relationship is pretty plain to see). But they are incorrect to see their children as reflections of themselves. Because they're not mirrors, they're human beings. They have their own strengths and weaknesses and they'll have to discover these for themselves on their journey to self-actualization (and beyond).

Furthermore, children can hardly be expected to reflect accurately on their parents because children are children and parents are adults. As we've seen, children have less intellect, less experience from which to learn and by which they may develop their skills and talents. For parents to hold children up to adult standards is not only absurd but it is doomed to fail. This often sets children on a course for various complexes and disorders.

But there are still (and often) occasions when parents are simply proactive, trying to instill in their children the drive to succeed, the willingness to risk failure, to be firmer at some times than at others. It's natural for parents to take a certain pride in their children, and to encourage their children to help contribute to that pride.

What's not natural (or healthy) is to fill your child with an overruling need to succeed, an unwillingness to accept failure, to be too firm at these times. Taking pride in your child is one thing, a healthy thing; taking pride only in their successes is not a healthy thing.

The narcissistic parent also tends to deny their child a secure sense of their own identity, their self-hood. And they do this through the development years and throughout their lives. The narcissistic parent needs the child, adult or minor, to be reliant upon them, never to abandon them. To achieve this, the child has to lack a certain self-confidence. It's the same way narcissists manipulate their prey on every level and strata of society. But parents are particularly well-suited and well-positioned to inflict this kind of manipulative control.

So, let's get into it. And don't be surprised if you notice a few of your own behaviors sneaking onto the list. Remember that a lot of narcissists don't even realize the damage they're doing.

Living vicariously is classic narcissistic parenting. This is where we see the first difference between proactive parenting and narcissistic. If the parent is acting on the child's behalf or for the child's benefit, that's parenting. It may be a bit parent-centric (if it's associated with something the parent does or did or enjoys), but it's hardly psychotic. When the effort is in the name of the parents' satisfaction and not the child, that's narcissistic. When parents are reliving their dreams through their children, seeing in the child a second chance of their own success, they are putting themselves at the center of their children's lives, to everybody's detriment. And crucially, when children are rejected for their failures, there is likely a narcissist at work. Because narcissists, you'll remember, have an ideal self-image. When the child's performance is considered part and parcel of that identity (their own, not the child's), the narcissist equates the child's failure with their own. The narcissist cannot abide failure if it's their own. The child is robbed of their self-hood and self-worth, their emotions and goals are devalued until they accept the role of an extension of the parent, not a fully-fledged person. This will keep the child in the parent's shadow for years to come, perhaps all of them.

Let's take a look at my own life for some interesting examples. I lived with my stepmother, whom I'll call Nancy, and my kid half-sister, whom I'll call Danielle. I lived with them and our father. Nancy was my father's third wife, my stepmother. You'll be reading a lot about my stepmother, a complicated and complex individual. Her experiences are good reminders that people are not merely collections of diagnosable traits, and that not every diagnosis includes every trait in the collected set.

For example, my stepmother was a pretty classic stage mother, putting my kid sister through years of dance classes and even into some modeling, things Nancy had pursued as a child. She also projected her lifetime's obsession with her own weight onto poor Danielle, who was developing eating complexes even as a child. Clearly, Nancy was living vicariously through her daughter, and this created a great deal of tension between the two. It wasn't that Danielle didn't enjoy dance classes, but there were conflicts between the two which were loud and terrible. They were too close for their mutual good. Nancy never gave Danielle her own space, let her develop her own identity, which brings us to that particular subject.

Marginalization is a word you may not know, but it means just what you'd think. When you marginalize someone, you shove them to the side (into the margins). This can happen in any number of ways. Ever give two weeks' notice at work? You're likely to be marginalized in that time, only because it's a part of the natural transition. An office or workplace is transitioning from one team member to the next. One in, one out; it's what it is. It happens in intimate relationships, unfortunately, and that can be a painful and revealing process. Being marginalized is never fun. It can fill someone with a sense of doubt, reduced worth or even worthlessness. Now imagine your parents doing it to you! It's sad, but it's what narcissists do, no matter who they're dealing with. Lovers, coworkers, friends; everybody has to take a backseat to the narcissist.

The problem is that it happens when the child is young, so it makes an indelible impression. And it comes from the person who has the most influence and the most responsibility for how a child is treated. So it's easy for a child to believe that he or she deserves to be marginalized, that they can't succeed against such competition.

On my mother's side of my divorced family was her husband, Willard, their daughter Robin, and my elder brothers Norris and Harry. Willard, my stepfather, was (like my stepmother) a complicated individual who brought to horrifying life the complexes and abuses we'll be looking at. In the case of marginalizing, we look to Willard for the example. And because I lived with my father (as the result of protracted custody battles) I was the one Willard marginalized. He did this in a variety of ways, both overt and covert. If you find yourself experiencing them or even exhibiting them yourself, take them very seriously.

One way Willard marginalized me was to ban me from his household. What happened was that, after years of custody battles, my mother offered to let me move to my father's house. I was in house of what I now know was full of narcissists to varying degrees, so it's little surprise that I wanted out in hindsight. She let me go, but I was never told that there was caveat; that was disallowed from coming back … ever, not even for a visit. My mother had been bluffing, she didn't think I'd go, so she failed to mention this.

I was nine years old.

At that time, I only saw my mother when she came to visit me to take me to dinners or movies, one day a week.

That's marginalizing on a pretty grand scale, but my guess is that it's not uncommon. And I'm sure if I could take a time machine to that time and have an adult conversation with him, things might have been different. But it was what it was. Later that year, as I came to understand, my half-sister on that side of the family missed me and wanted to invite me to her birthday party, at which time my stepfather relented.

Marginalizing was only one narcissistic trait Willard exhibited, among several complexes and abuses.

This brings us to two mindsets which are at the heart of many conditions, complexes, and disorders. Most things about a person's way of thinking come down to one's mindset; either growth-minded or fixed minded. Developed early in life, the fixed mindset believes that patterns recur in life, that people are either winners or losers; winners win, losers lose. The success or failure of their efforts equate to their failure or success as a human being. They often learn this in childhood from parents who fail to instill them with a growth mindset. The growth-minded person accepts failure as a part of the process of success, externalizes their identity from their achievements, and they believe that nothing is fixed.

Narcissistic parents may nit-pick, engage in passive-aggressive insults or backhanded compliments such as:

- "You're so talented. It's a pity you don't take care of your appearance."
- "You're really quite pretty for a girl of your weight."
- "It's not your fault, you just don't have that certain element."
- "If anybody's interested in you, it's for one thing and one thing only … and it's not going to be your talent."

Willard liked to say I'd be bald before I was twenty-one. I didn't happen, but it's easy to see how reductive that was, and how deliberate. I was a little overweight, and he once said at a party, to his friends, "He looks just like his mother … breasts and everything."

Let's take another look at grandiosity and superiority. Here we're not referring to the clinical use of *grandiose,* as in a narcissism diagnosis. We mean, well, grandiosity. Narcissistic parents are often prone to histrionic performances, exhibitionistic behavior, always drawing attention to themselves. They feel naturally superior and they expect to be treated as such. The problem with this as a trait in parents is that kids are cute and precocious and naturally draw people's attentions. They say the darndest things. They're natural attention magnets. And that seriously threatens the narcissistic parent. They have to compete all the harder and marginalize all the more to secure their place at the forefront of everybody's attention. Just as a narcissist is likely to use another person, either a friend or coworker or partner, as tools to fortify their narcissistic world view, the parent makes a tool of their child. The children are often instilled with the same sense of superiority and entitlement their parents have. This superiority is rarely earned by actual achievement by the child, as it is with the parents. It's often associated more with material trappings than any superiority of ideals or virtue.

The superficial image is a big part of all this grandiosity. Nothing replaces the show of admiration and affection. For the narcissist, it's like a narcotic to which they are addicted. It doesn't matter what generates that admiration; their house, their car, their money, their kids. All are just totems to their excellence, after all.

And just as narcissists engage in marginalizing competition with their kids, they do the same thing with friends and fellow parents. They delight in one-upping the others, exhibiting the best and most expensive things, and the most proficient and powerful children. They seek envy, and to do that they have to reduce the others. Remember how transactional the narcissist's frame of mind is.

This can take a unique and terrible manifestation when two parents divorce. As we'll see, narcissistic stepparents often have a very strong sense of competition with the husband or wife they're replacing.

But the divorced birth parents can be just as competitive against the other. This can come in any number of forms. One parent may try to one-up the other in terms of lavish gifts, expensive vacations (if the courts allow it), bigger homes. Divorced parents compete for their child's admiration and attention in this way, and it can set a terrible example to the child or children. They may become entitled, spoiled, and begin mirroring the other narcissistic behaviors, which we know are learned and develop through life.

This is even more likely when you take a few other things into account. A divorce is often called a *failed marriage*, and that's an unfortunate turn of phrase. It intimates that one person failed the other, failed themselves, and failed the child. There can be great guilt and responsibility after a divorce between both birth parents, and that can result in spoiling the child. They failed the child and both parents are bound to know how difficult it can be for a child. The child may have feelings of having failed, of being lost. Guilty parents may go to great lengths (too far, often times) in trying to make it up to their children. Sadly, they're often doing more harm than good.

We've already seen how manipulative the narcissist can be. They use guilt, martyrdom, and victimhood to perfection. Observe:

- "I gave you everything, the best years of my life!" (guilt)
- "If it weren't for you, everything would have been different." (shame)
- "I was so embarrassed in front of my friends!" (responsibility)
- "Why can't you be more like your father/mother/sister/brother/cousin/friend?" (unfair comparison)
- "Don't you dare embarrass me again!" (unreasonable pressure)
- "You'll do it or I'm cutting you off!" (contingent reward and punishment)
- "What did I do to deserve such a son/daughter?" (emotional coercion)

Note that these all have something in common; love as a bartering tool. It's either offered with contingencies as a reward, or denied as a punishment. Neither of my birth parents did this to me or my brothers, but each of my stepparents did treat their own birthchildren this way. My stepfather bemoaning having sacrificed his career to care for my half-sister, Robin, who had special needs due to a head injury. Actually, he lost his career to alcoholism. But he was happy to boast about his sacrifice.

Being inflexible and overly sensitive are hallmarks of narcissism, and they're even worse when in a parenting situation. Their expectations and rules can be rigid and demanding. They'll claim it's to create disciplined children, but nothing the narcissist really has anything to do with anybody else. The truth is that they're dedicated to themselves in every way, and that includes their rules. Their need for obedience applies especially to their children. And they become quicky irritated with their children, leaving them confused and in doubt. A narcissistic parent will cite disobedience, perceived shortcomings, bad timing, or lack of attention or attentiveness on the child's part.

Again, let's look at my stepmother, but not her relationship with me (that's for the chapter about narcissistic stepparents). But Nancy's behavior and relationship with her own natural-born daughter Danielle. Nancy became greatly frustrated when her daughter was disobedient. Let me point out at this point that my father, older when Danielle was born, stayed out of the parenting, something we'll discuss later. So Nancy and Danielle were left to face off one against the other; a forty-year-old narcissist and her ten-year-old daughter. Nancy favored books about parenting, and would often bluff her daughter to create her compliance.

Nancy might say something like, "Do it or I'll take you out of dance class!"

To which Danielle's quick and simple reply would be something like, "Fine, I don't even like dance class."

Nancy would soon escalate things, until toys were being thrown out of the room, piling up against my bedroom door. Next were the dresses and other clothes. I can still remember the shouting, my kid sister screaming for my help, my stepmother saying grimly to me, "Don't you dare open that door!"

Good times.

Seriously, though, it's proof positive and a clear illustration of how a narcissist's need to be obeyed can take shape in the household, even among parents and their blood-children.

Lack of empathy comes up again and again in this field of study, and for good reason. The narcissist lacks empathy, which is a key element in emotional intelligence and social skills. The fact that some people just can't find it anywhere inside them is tragic, to be frank. These people may spend their lives suspecting something is wrong but they can't be sure what.

In a parenting situation, this means understanding a child's different needs and abilities. It means considering their dreams and desires and not the parent's own frustrated history or stunted future. This is one of the narcissist parent's most costly mistakes. Because empathy can be nurtured in children, and it truly ought to be. Foregoing that, parents leave their children in an emotional and social wasteland; unable to connect to anybody but themselves and, by wicked design, their parents.

This can inspire three separate responses. The children may rebel and stand up against their parents. They may flee and disconnect from their parents (the two equal parts of the famed *fight or flight* response). The third response it to freeze, paralyzed by incomprehensible truths an a world they can't quite understand and definitely can't relate to.

We're going to take a closer look at dependency/codependency. But it does belong here as a common behavior or narcissistic parents. Codependent relationships are signaled when one partner enables the abusive or antisocial behavior of the other. In this context, the abusive parents want their kids to enable them, take care of them for the rest of their lives. And there is a certain twisted kind of logic to this. There is a social construct which establishes that, in an ideal society, parents take care of their children and then children take care of their elders. It's prevalent in Latin and Asian countries. Some countries, like the United States, marginalize their elderly, tossing them into convalescent hospitals to die a lonesome, neglected death. So it's not surprising that parents would have some instinctive investment in their children's success.

And while it's great to have successful adult children who can support their parents through retirement, it's just not as common. In 2020, the millennials are the first American generation to fail to exceed their parents' level of accomplishment. And for an adult to live in the expectation of being supported is congruous at best. After all, children don't ask to be born. Parents raise their children because they want to and because they have to. The children owe the parents nothing other than respect and a certain level of obedience. But to shoulder them with the responsibility of their parents' retirement is both unrealistic and selfish. It's like having a baby in order to save your marriage. A baby's not a marriage counselor and it's not a retirement IRA account.

It's just another part of the neediness, the fear of abandonment, the fear of shattering their idealized self-image. And to do this, a parent may go to great lengths; discouraging risk taking and asking unreasonable sacrifices.

Possessiveness and jealousy are very common for the narcissistic parent. This is because they've invested their narcissistic needs in their children. Any threat to that cannot be tolerated. The child's growing independence will present endless opportunities for the child to grow and change and betray their parents' unrealistic expectations.

A romantic partner may be particularly threatening and may come under unrealistic and unreasonable scrutiny. Sadly, this can also contaminate the child's view of the partner, of any potential partner. Snide comments and insults and judgments not only destroy relationships, but create a false sense of superiority in the child. This perpetuates the child's own idealized self-image and contributes to their lifelong isolation and a series of failed relationships. Sadly, that's just what the narcissistic parent wants.

Neglect is extremely common in narcissistic parenting. As much as the narcissist enjoys power over their children, as important as that power is in their long-term campaign, there are other things competing for the narcissistic parent's attention; namely, themselves. Self-gratification can take many forms, from the attention of others or a grandiose celebration, perfect for exhibitionism. These often distract the narcissistic parent, resulting in their children's neglect. This can lead to narcissism both grandiose and vulnerable.

A narcissistic parent may deny their children necessities, requiring that they be earned. This is a way for the parent to control the child and to assert and ingrain that sense of control. Since parents are the gatekeepers of a child's life, they can control how much the children are allowed to eat, drink, even to sleep. They may also withhold love, affection, praise, things children need to flourish. Different than neglect, denial entails deliberate withholding based on a transactional demand; obedience in exchange for an evening meal, for example.

Neglect often takes a more overt shape, however, and it often happens in cases of foster parenting. Children may be left to live in squalor, surrounded by filth, eating rotting food if any, ravaged by parasites and disease. These children, often several per household, are often left to look after one another. They are not given adequate healthcare and are often not sent to school. This type of neglect is physical (not merely psychological) and so it is considered criminal child abuse in all US fifty United States and elsewhere in the free world to varying degrees.

This brings me to my father, Harvey. Harvey was not what I would consider a narcissist. He had no need to be adored, he had considerable empathy, he was not inflexible in most ways. But my father did neglect his last child, Danielle. Her every needs were seen too, of course, she was not left in want of anything. In fact, her mother Nancy spoiled her. But my father hadn't wanted another child. Divorced with aging sons, he wasn't interested in raising another child late in life. He also wasn't interested in being alone for the rest of his life. He liked Nancy and knew she wanted a child, so they struck a kind of unspoken bargain. He got the wife he wanted, she got the daughter she wanted.

But the result of this was that my father didn't engage in raising, punishing, or guiding his daughter. It wasn't his best move, as it left the girl without a sufficient male role model. My father was busy working.

He did take them on vacations and the like, of course. He wasn't an absentee parent. But there was a kind of invisible line of participation which he wouldn't cross. It left her spoiled and him often frustrated. It was also, it should be said, unfair to Nancy. True, she knew what she was getting into, and raising her daughter was the absolute center of her life. But she was in over her head and spent a lot of time flailing just to keep from going under in a number of ways.

It just goes to show that these things can be incremental, in the vast gray area of life instead of in the extreme margins.

Parentification, (also called *enmeshment* or *covert incest*) can occur as children get older, and involves a kind of romanticizing or even sexualizing of the relationship. This may happen with fathers and their teenage daughters. If the father isolates the daughter and properly manipulates her to give him unquestioning adoration, this kind of dynamic is shockingly easy to allow to occur. It's damaging to the daughter, who may wind up with the Electra complex among others. She may never feel comfortable in an age-appropriate relationship, and even older men will fail to match the idealized image of the sexualized father figure.

Preferential treatment among children is a very common type of psychological child abuse. One child is singled out either for better treatment or one for worse. Often, one will be preferred while the other is treated especially poorly or ignored. It may be quite subtle, just enough to register with both children on a subconscious level, which is just what the narcissist prefers. Both children are being taught what place they hold in the house and what place they'll go on to have in society. This is when and how the seeds of grandiose and vulnerable narcissism are planted.

Incessant humiliation and teasing can have terrible effects on a child. A little kidding around is good, to teach a child how to take a joke, to laugh at themselves. That leads them to greater emotional intelligence and social skills. But, as with so many things, it's a matter of proportion. Too much of this so-called parenting technique breaks down a child's sense of self, their identity. It's especially bad when combined with preferential or exclusionary treatment.

This brings me to my own relationship with my mother, Bonnie. Good woman that she is, and not notably a narcissist as far as I can reliably diagnose (and I'm something of an expert, twice published on the subject), this facet of narcissism did creep into our relationship. It's quite common in parenting, I would say, which makes it all the more insidious.

The first thing to note is that her favorite was always the eldest of the three boys, Harry. I think it's pretty common for the firstborn to have special place in a parent's heart. Perhaps it's because of the relationship they've created, which is extremely dysfunctional due to his antisocial personality disorder. Either way, he's her favorite.

As a third-born son, I think the bloom may have been off the parenting rose by the time I came around. That, I imagine, is also quite common. But when I left her house to live with my father, even though she opened that door, things changed. She didn't withhold her love, she didn't become antagonistic. There was nothing covert ever about her behavior. But thereafter she was quick to make little jabs, be vaguely insulting in a way she wouldn't be to my brothers or our half-sister. She would always take her daughter's side against mine (likely due to the girl's brain injury and the guilt associated with that). But I was almost left off the guest list to my own grandfather's funeral, so there's that.

Privacy violations are a heavy to blow to kids, and a common manner of parental psychological abuse. Kids take that to heart. All they really have is their privacy, that's the one thing they might feel that they could (and should) be able to control. Violating this destroys trust and engenders resentment, suspicion, and inspires similar behavior by the child later in life. This person will spy on their lovers, stalk their exes, disrespect everybody they come across. Their relationships will fail, and they may face a life of lonely isolation. Reading a child's diary, for example, or going through their drawers, is likely going to be a mistake. A parent may justify it as a drug search, but without a history of that, nobody will believe it and they probably shouldn't. This behavior may indicate paranoid personality disorder on the part of the parent and could nurture paranoia in the child.

Threats of physical violence are common to abusive parents. Many will justify it as long as there is no actual violence, but that doesn't reverse the psychological damage which gets done, and that can be considerable. The threat always looms, it could come out of nowhere. This creates insecurity, anxiety, stress, and mistrust.

Narcissistic parents will often make two children compete for their love and approval. This exaggerated favoritism does more than reward one and punish the other, it creates hostility between the two siblings, hostility which may linger for a lifetime. This abuse not only damages the relationship between the siblings, it can damage the relationships between parents and children. And this can be done simply by comparing the two unnecessarily, praising the one to the other, goading one on to dominate the other and the other to resist domination. It's about a divide-and-conquer method of controlling at least one of the children. But that's enough to keep them from uniting against the parent later, which is what the narcissist fears most.

There's no religious family abuse *per se*, but this falls under the heading of identity abuse, making a person question everything about themselves, including their ideals and belief sets. Parents who use the concept of God as the ultimate punisher for their misdeeds is utterly terrifying, considering how much power God has in the eyes of a small child. Comparisons may also be made to Judas, Jezebel, and some of the less-savory figures in both testaments. It's an abuse of the children and an abuse of the religious concepts.

Divorce can be painful, for the kids even more than the parents. But narcissistic parents can't focus on anybody's pain but their own. So when kids are caught in the middle, parents can unleash some terribly destructive abuses. Corrupting a child's view of the other parent, insulting them, breaking down that relationship, is a terrible and selfish practice. It does have a high success rate, because children are impressionable, because narcissists are charming and manipulative, and because the corruption happens with the other can't do or say anything about it. By the time the parent in question has a chance to change the misimpression, it could be too late. This behavior may destroy relationships between children and parents, and it may create an unwillingness on the child's part to have a family later in life for fear of being victimized in this way after the divorce.

This was a staple of my post-divorce childhood. My mother and stepfather ridiculed our father and tried to marginalize him in our eyes. The way my father would say the words, "Your mother," with such undisguised disdain, was both passive-aggressive and verbally abusive, and I'm pretty sure he knew that.

Narcissistic parents enjoy playing the victim while blaming the child. They use guilt to manipulate their children and secure their loyalty.

Narcissistic parents won't allow a child to communicate clearly what they need. They'll either marginalize, compare, or use other time-tested devices to end the conversation. They may use guilt and shame to turn it back around on the child, with such responses as, "It's always about you, isn't it? I just don't want to hear anymore of this!" Threats of violence or other punishment won't be far behind, just for the crime of self-expression. This can stifle a person for a lifetime, create vulnerable narcissists, victim and guilt personality disorders.

Emotion-shaming may seem to some parents like a good idea, but that's misguided. Children are more emotional and less rational than adults, and these parents are lacking empathy, they can't see the situation from their child's perspective. Crying or having hurt feelings may be appropriate or not depending on the circumstances. But it's never appropriate to shame the child. Parents should have the good sense to externalize, separate the person from the behavior. Emotions pass, learning opportunities come and go. But the child is your child for life. Narcissists lose sight of this and their kids pay the price.

Violating age-appropriate boundaries could signal other abuses which may be looming or already in play. In this type of behavior, a parent may assert their right to watch an age-inappropriate child, to undress, calling it a parent's right, or attentive parenting. Of course, given the genders in question, this could be voyeurism bordering on sexual abuse. Other age-appropriate boundaries may include so-called *helicopter parenting* (unnecessary intervention in interpersonal conflicts), social restrictions, restricting finances and mobility.

Parental entitlement is a particularly insidious type of psychological abuse. Parents feel they have a right to their child's dedication, using guilt and shame to manipulate them. A mother, who gives a special portion of physical devotion to the child even before it's born, may be partial to this device, but fathers can use it too: "This is the way you treat me, after carrying you for nine months! My body was never the same! Did I shoulder you with a stepfather? And this is the thanks I get?" From one's father, they might hear complaints about years of hard work, money spent in education, other sacrifices. Narcissistic parents feel that these sacrifices earn them the devotion they crave.

Narcissistic child abusers also favor invalidation as a psychological device to reduce their sense of self and self-worth. If you've ever heard a parent say to their child something like, "You don't know what trouble is! When I was a kid ..." or perhaps, "It could have been worse! I'll give you something to cry about," then you've come across invalidation. It reduces the victim's feelings, concerns, self-image, it reduces the victim in every way. It's a classic marginalization technique, only it marginalizes the child's feelings and experiences instead of themselves. It's not as big a step in the right direction as you may think.

Child abuse can take on a financial aspect as well. Of course, parents control how much spending power a child has, and that's reasonable. Children lack the intellectual capacity to be left in full control of their own money, if they have any. It's for good, conscientious parents to save for their children, to teach them how to save and spend wisely on their own. But the narcissistic parent won't do that. Why? Because money means freedom, even in tiny increments; the power to make choices and live with them, the power to save or invest or indulge themselves. But power in the hands of the victim is the enemy of the narcissistic parent. Power is the last thing they want their children to have, to get used to, to crave. So controlling money is a great way for the narcissistic parent to control their child. They may do this by confiscating any earned money, birthday money, anything. They may claim it is to put the money aside, but this is predicably rare. More often than not, the parent keeps and spends the money, justifying it as being a good lesson for the child about the hardness of life, and as a way to contribute to the household after years of being a financial burden. Parents may go further, forging signatures to clean out bank accounts. They may get credit cards in their children's names, which is credit card fraud in most cases. They can then charge up the cards, default, and let their children deal with the fallout. It will only hobble them financially, which is just what the narcissistic parent would want. It gives them total control. What's more, the child may never know it was their parent who took the illegal card out in the first place, so long as they manage to get away with it.

Infamous Cases

It's an unfortunate truth that official criminal records all over the world reflect horrific cases of child abuse, at the hands of their parents, teachers, friends. This book focuses on the child-parent relationship, so we'll keep our focus on that for now. Still, there are cases you may have heard of and some which may surprise you. You might be shocked to learn that some of your own heroes are survivors of child abuse at the hands of their parents. Let them impress and inspire you all over again!

But keep something in mind: These are famous people who overcame abuse to succeed. Their experiences may resonate. But don't misconstrue this as an indirect equation of abuse equals success. More often than not, is can guarantee failure. These are the exceptions to the vast and horrific rule that childhood abuses, especially at the hands of parents, can be life-crushing.

Acting legend Marlon Brando, a sex symbol and revolutionary actor of the 1950s, and comeback kid of the 1970s, admitted in his autobiography to being abused by his father. The abuse was verbal, psychological, and physical. It haunted the actor throughout his life, creating in him a crippling hero complex which had him expending his energies on others' causes instead of his own personal relationships. His fractured family and the premature deaths of his children attest to the damage which can linger as the result of parental abuse, particularly psychological.

Actress Drew Barrymore, of the famous Barrymore dynasty of actors, reportedly suffered abuse at the hands of her father John. Though she, like Brando, still went on to achieve great things, her notorious adolescent likely had clear ties to that abuse. It's likely that she was breaking free of it and into a premature adulthood facilitated by her wealth and fame and enabled by sycophants around her in those formidable years.

Talk show legend Oprah Winfrey has apparently been open about the sexual abuse she suffered as a child, and has gone on to lend her incredible wealth, celebrity, power, talents, and energy to helping others face their own challenges of this sort.

Pop singer Christina Aguilera is reported to be the victim of physical and emotional abuse by her father and has reportedly cut her father off, ten years running. There's an example of a successful disengagement from a parent. She took her position and held her ground.

Legendary sex symbol Marylin Monroe was a foster child and is said to have been sexually abused by her lovers. She was one of the first celebrities to talk about such things openly, making her a pioneer in a field which still needs to be filled by more volunteers brave enough to come forward and shed light on this crippling set of behaviors.

Contemporary comic filmmaker Tyer Perry is reported to have been physically abused by his father and also sexually abused by other adults during his earlier years. Comic and TV personality Rosie O'Donnell reportedly claims that she and her siblings endured a variety of concurrent abuses. Comic actress Roseanne Barr is said to have been sexually abused during childhood, which could easily have had an impact on her publicly troubled marriage to fellow comic Tom Arnold. Folksinger Jewel Kilcher was reportedly physically and mentally abused by her father, and famously spend her pre-fame adult years living in a car. Actress and musician Queen Latifah is reportedly the victim of childhood sexual abuse.

Saturday Night Live's Chevy Chase has openly discussed being locked in a closet for hours by his mother and stepfather, only to be beaten before being released. He's Chevy Chase and you're not … bet you're glad of that now. From the same show, Darrell Hammond has publicly discussed physical (and horrific) abuses he suffered at the hands of his mother. Author Rudyard Kipling was reportedly tortured by his caregivers as a child.

These abuses aren't always physical, mental, or sexual. Superstar entertainer Britney Spears continues to wrestle with father Jamie Spears over control of her considerable fortune. Decades earlier, Charlie Chaplin's *The Kid* costar Jackie Coogan's parents absconded with his childhood fortune. His lawsuit against them established the so-called *Coogan Law*, which protects money earned by children from their parents.

The abused party, of course, is not always the future celebrity. Others may rise to become abusers of note. Joan Crawford's daughter Christine's memoir Mommy Dearest, made into a film only a few years later, details horrific physical and mental abuses from the classically narcissistic star of the silver screen. The elder Crawford's other abuses reportedly include substance and sexual abuses.

Outside the entertainment world, US President Bill Clinton admits to being raised by an alcoholic, exposing him to related abuses. Former first lady Eleanor Roosevelt never spoke of it, as befitted the temper of her times, but she's widely believed to have been abused at home. Disgraced US President Richard Nixon reported suffered deprivation (neglect) and physical abuse during his evangelical Quaker upbringing in Yorba Linda, California. Gloria Steinem is reported to have been neglected by her father during her childhood after her mother's mental breakdown and her father's abandonment.

The rare instance of celebrity prolicide (the act of murdering one's own child) are also limited to cases like the aforementioned soul singer Marvin Gaye and his father, who shot the singer dead in 1884. It's important to remember that murder, of whatever sort, is distinct from abuse of any sort; murder is a one-time act by its very nature, and abuse is a prolonged or chronic state of repeated behaviors. History gives us such infamous child-murders such as Ivan the Terrible (who killed his namesake son), Peter the Great (who killed his son, Alexei), and Nazi Chief of Propaganda Joseph Goebbels, who (along with his wife) poisoned all six of their young children during the fall of Berlin in 1945.

But, as we said, these abuses can go in different and unexpected directions. Let's flip the coin of parent/child abuse and inspect its dexter side, when children abuse their parents.

CHAPTER FOUR: Narcissistic and Abusive Adult Children

Now we go from child abuse (abuse of children by parents) to parent abuse, the abuse of parents by their teenage or adult children. Physical, financial, and psychological abuses are the most common from child to parent.

Both types of abuse are considered family abuse, which may also include spousal abuse and others. Parent abuse is often found alongside other antisocial behaviors such as substance abuse.

While parent abuse can take a number of different forms, they most commonly involve the mother as the victim, and often include perpetrators who are under 18 years old. And the term *child-to-parent violence*, used in many such cases, is simply too vague. Violence doesn't include psychological or financial abuse, two common forms of parent abuse. At the same time, some children and early teens may swat at their parents without it being considered either violence or abuse.

Incidents of CPV and parent abuse may be on the rise for a number of cultural reasons. The current generation was raised with new, progressive, and lenient approaches unknown to previous generations. For the first time, kids were given trophies just for participating, nobody could be made to feel slighted. This politically correct culture surely had some positive effects on interracial tolerance, but it created an entire generation who were raised to believe they always won, no matter what; and that they never lost, no matter what. This has created a narcissistic bent to the generation, entitlement and superiority being hallmarks of their behavior. Add to this a general failure to find gainful employment in society, poise them for financial and other abuses.

At the same time, parents get old and sick and vulnerable. Once the victim, the child has grown into a narcissist in their own right. We've already seen how narcissism is a learned set of behaviors, and that set is learned principally from parents. Now those same parents become the victims of the next generation of narcissists. They're marginalized, they're manipulated, made to suffer abuses just as they were made to in their own childhoods, and often by the same hands which reach out to them in need.

There's another dynamic to consider. Very often it is the father who is the perpetrator of physical and sexual abuse, in particular. Years later, in the absence of that parent (often by death), the mother is the so-called *last man standing*. Of course, any parent who stands by and allows abuses to occur must carry their portion of the blame. Silence is violence, as they now say. But in some cases, the surviving mother may have to bear the brunt of her late husband's abuses.

Interestingly, the son-to-mother abusive relationship parallels the basic framework of male-to-female abusive relationships. Race doesn't seem to be an issue in this kind of abuse.

The effects of CPV and parent abuse can be devastating. It's been found to impact physical and mental health, with stress factors such as shame, fear, despair, and guilt being commonly reported. These feelings can have physiological effects on the body, including sudden inflammation and adrenaline which can lead to heart attack or stroke. Long-term psychological health is also under threat from isolation, depression, self-doubt, and may lead to corrosion of the sense of self the elderly need as their intellectual faculties begin to fail them.

Criminalization of parent abuse falls along the lines of physical abuse cases. Psychological, financial, or identity abuses narcissistic children may inflict aren't really crimes. And in a lot of cases the so-called perpetrators are minors and beyond serious prosecution, especially for actions that aren't even criminal.

But there are a number of therapies to correct this, if both parties are willing. We'll look at that in greater detail in a later section of this book. We looked at ending abusive relationships, and at some point it will behoove the physically abused parent to separate themselves from the child. But as it was with the reverse situation years before, the elder may be codependent on the adult child for finances, for help getting food, for all manner of assistance. Just cutting them out may not be so easy. What's worse, the parent may be racked with feelings of guilt, that they deserve the treatment they're getting, developing guilt and victim complexes to accent their previous, perhaps grandiose narcissism.

There are also sentimental considerations. Hard as it may be for an adult child to cut out an abusive parent from their lives, it can be even harder for a parent (a mother especially) to cut out an adult child. It's their compulsion to forgive, to nurture, regardless of past transgressions. And the pain of abuse from a child to a mother must surely be the worst betrayal a person can feel, especially a former (or current) narcissist.

Infamous Cases

The 1989 murder of José and Mary Menendez at the hands of their sons, Lyle and Eric, captured the public's attention, as did the Lizzie

Borden murders of her parents of over a century before. The Menendez boys were convicted, Borden was not. The Menendez boys claimed abuse as motive for the murders, though this remains arguable. Borden pled not guilty to the charge of a double murder of her father and stepmother. And since the murders in both cases were swift and brutal, it's hard to distinguish them as parent abuse and not parricide (the murder of both parents).

Unfortunately, many cases of parent abuse go unreported. Parents resist criminalizing their children, and the children don't just turn themselves in (virtually impossible for a narcissist, parent or child).

Now another manifestation of narcissism which must not be ignored. We learn things like narcissism from our parents (though the lessons don't always take). Still, siblings of a narcissistic upbringing are likely to face terrible challenges. It can be a perfect storm for a narcissistic abusive relationship. If you're dealing with a narcissistic sibling, or you've accused of being (or suspect you may be) one yourself, read on. You may not like what you learn, about yourself or someone who is close to you. But like the Old Testament story of Cain and Abel, narcissism between brothers can be devastating and even deadly.

CHAPTER FIVE:
Narcissistic Siblings

Adam and Eve, to remind you, had two mortal sons called Cain (the eldest, a farmer) and Abel (the younger, rancher). Both make sacrifices to God, and God is more pleased with Abel's sacrifice. Cain feigns friendliness until he and Abel are out in the field before striking at him in ambush and killing him.

It's the first murder of the Hebrew race (some would say). But what is inarguable is that it is a classic instance of narcissistic siblings and the damage such a relationship can reap. The elements of Caine's narcissistic personality disorder are clear. He's radically insecure, cannot tolerate any position other than first, blameful of others, unable to accept responsibility, desperate for love and admiration. He lacks empathy for his brother, or his still-living parents who are about to lose a child. He cares only for himself and serves only himself. He's charming and duplicitous and manipulating. He sees the sacrifice in a transactional manner, as the praise Abel receives is seen by Caine as necessarily taken away from him. He is fearful of abandonment by God. He is histrionic and must be the center of attention. He his grandiose in his sacrifice and in his revenge. He lashes out in sudden and uncontrollable rage.

While we're mainly concerned with the narcissistic relationships between parents and children, we're only hobbling our own complete understanding of the entirety of the condition if we skip the fascinating and frightening world of narcissistic sibling.

It only makes sense. We've seen how narcissism is a learned set of behaviors, and so two or more children are more than likely to be raised in the same household and with the same set of influences. Not only are budding narcissists created via this twisted model, but it's only inevitable that the siblings would turn their narcissistic tendencies against each other. And since siblings are never identical (even when they're so-called *identical twins*), we can imagine (and research proves it) that narcissistic siblings inflict the same kind of damage and provide the same kind of complicated threats to self-care as other familial narcissistic cases of parents and children.

As it is with all narcissists, the narcissistic sibling exhibits the classic needs of narcissism: Lack of empathy, need for unquestioned adoration and loyalty, exhibitionism, fear of abandonment, need for control. But in this case, one sibling turns that need for control and admiration and loyalty toward the other sibling.

Why not? Chances are that, if two children are raised under narcissistic parents, both have been indoctrinated in the ways of narcissism in one way or the other. Depending on age and temperament, the children may naturally gravitate toward one type of narcissism or the other, or develop supplemental complexes; victim complex to the other's hero complex, guilt to God, inferiority to superiority complex.

It often fits the narcissistic parent's agenda, to turn the children against each other, to treat one as superior and one as inferior. It's as if the narcissistic parent was deliberately creating an imbalance, and of course they are. We're already seen how narcissistic parents use a divide-and-conquer method of controlling both children, each for the parent's own benefit. Creating a natural-born grandiose narcissist and another child with a ready-made guilt complex is the perfect equation to create a secure and controlling narcissistic parent.

Narcissistic siblings have complimentary and supplementary motives for their actions. The dominant or abusive sibling hopes to control their sibling for their own security, as their parents did. But they also hope to win the narcissistic parents' love and approval, most likely contingent upon success. The other sibling, submissive, can only hope to win the parents' sympathy, or anybody else's if they can. And both children will manifest the results of their upbringing, following the sad paths set forth for them by their parents' behavior.

Sibling narcissism is useful for the narcissist because it provides a ready-made victim who may consider themselves honor-bound to accept the treatment, as they might have with a parent. In fact, the narcissistic sibling resembles the narcissistic parent in just about every way. An older sibling even as the natural authority which a parent may have established in years past.

But, as equals and sharing childhood protocols, a narcissistic sibling may have advantages over the victim sibling which even adults do not have. Unlike anyone else, for example, a sibling (especially an older sibling) has access to the victim, as they likely are growing up in the same house. The narcissistic sibling may then manipulate the victim sibling in any number of ways, and manipulation is key to the narcissist's functionality.

The narcissistic sibling may use any one of the abuses or complexes we've discussed. To wit:

The narcissist sibling (not always older) may convince the victim that they're the best of friends, that mutual loyalty is the bedrock of their friendship.

But they have no true friendship based on mutual respect. As the adult narcissist does with fellow adults, the child narcissist sibling lies and presents an idealized image to manipulate the victim. As a sibling, it's easy to engender and to demand both trust and loyalty. One thing the narcissistic sibling can claim as a qualifier of control which no outside narcissist can claim is the family bond. Who can argue with that? Well, we know that's just what the narcissist wants, a position where there is no reasonable argument against unquestioned support and adoration and obedience. They say blood is thicker than water; well, narcissists scream it.

Along these lines, a narcissistic sibling is especially well-positioned in another way. They know their sibling better than others. So they know where the vulnerabilities to manipulation are. They know the victim's needs and desires and they can appeal to them, no matter how legitimate or authentic the appeals may be. It's about emotional manipulation as much if not more than rational. They also know where the victim's strengths are, so they'll know what areas are manipulative blind alleys. Narcissism is particularly effective for siblings in this way. And it's particularly cruel given the natural responsibility of one sibling to another, mirroring the responsibilities of parents to children; to nurture, to protect, to enrich and to support.

A narcissistic sibling will likely use this bond to turn the sibling into a living pincushion, a device for expressing their inner turmoil, a punching bag incarnate. And the other sibling, more often than not, will have been trained from childhood simply to take it. That shoulders the victim with a guilt complex at the very least, and can lead to a fixed mindset, low or no self-esteem, depression, and other related and oft-deadly complications.

An even uglier side of sibling narcissism comes, as we've already seen, when one form of abuse overlaps with or leads to another. Male narcissistic siblings may become predatory or develop all manner of disorders when manipulating female siblings (or step-siblings, very often the case). This may dovetail with physical, sexual, and psychological abuses, of which only the first two may be considered criminal (or worthy of prosecution) in the United States in 2021.

Dealing with a Narcissistic Sibling

Sadly, the same limited options open to dealing with any other narcissist applies to a sibling. Depending on the severity of the behaviors, the progression of the illness, and the willingness of the sufferer, corrective measures may include psychotherapy and medication. A family intervention may be necessary in the case of substance abuse, a way to manage a concurrent disorder while trying to manage what may be an untreatable condition.

Otherwise, you can declare, convince, establish boundaries until the cows come home, it probably won't do any good.

Failing management or treatment, one may have to cut loose of their narcissistic sibling. This may be challenging, but it will be easier than dividing from your parents (depending). As adults, you likely live apart (hopefully), perhaps even in different cities or states or even countries. True, you may have shared interests, including family businesses such as investments and inheritances and care of other family members. But remember that you can always interact with such a personality on a superficial level, just enough to accomplish what needs to be accomplished, without opening yourself up to any unnecessary manipulation.

If you feel you have to do this, how to do it best? We'll touch on this in more in a later section of this book, but for now let's look to our standbys: Emotional intelligence and social skills. Find a quiet place and time, prepare your thoughts and know your needs and desires, communicate clearly, have a plan and stick to it.

Signs of a Narcissistic Sibling

Sibling relationships can be complicated; in fact, they always are. So it's not always easy to identify a narcissistic sibling from a merely domineering one. Take a look at these qualifiers and see if your own sibling (or yourself) measures up to the diagnosis.

Do you enjoy your sibling's company? Don't discount your emotional core reactions. Your reasoning, rational self may find justifications for excusal or acceptance, but that's just what the narcissistic sibling (or any narcissist) is counting on. Emotions are trickier to decipher, but they're far more honest as far as our instincts are concerned. If you just don't like the person nature shouldered you with, there may well be a reason, or several. Plumb those depths, don't be afraid of the answers or even the questions.

The bottom line is this; you can choose your friends but you can't choose your family. You can, however, which members of your family are actually friends. They're distinct and different. Family are the people you knew first, the people you have genetic connections. You can't change that. Friends are people with whom you share values, affection, and respect. You can be friends with one brother and not another, for instance, or with one parent or not the other. That depends on who you are as adults, not who gave birth to whom or when.

Of my two brothers, one of them is (I'm sorry to say) a sufferer of antisocial personality disorder, or sociopathy. It happened over the course of his life, developing from narcissist to narcissistic personality disorder, complicated by a sadistic quality. He also engages in every type of abuse and has a number of complexes. So he'll be coming up a lot in this chapter about narcissistic adult siblings.

Along these lines, take a close look at your own sibling's (or siblings') methods of communication.

Are they clear and concise about their needs and desires, or are they vague and circular in their logic? Do they employ the manipulative powers to make you doubt yourself? Do you walk away from conflicts doubting yourself or your belief systems? Do you feel confused or uncertain? Does every conversation become an interrogation by some paranoid conspiracy theorist putting you on the theoretical stand of their cross-examination? That's not a friendship and it's not a healthy relationship for anyone outside of a courtroom, where you both may wind up eventually.

My relationship with my brother checks every box. He goes on and on about conspiracy theories about the fidelity of his ex-wife, turning conversations into interrogations. He's quick to become enraged and act out (classic narcissism) but then will suddenly shift gears to become almost theatrically reasonable. Once he's manipulated the other into anger, he ducks back and plays the role of the calm, reasonable one. But this is only after he's incited the anger. Whether this is more strategic than bi-polar is hard to say, but the effect is much the same. It's a form of gaslighting, but it didn't work on me. Don't let it work on you. If you find yourself doing it, check yourself. It's blatantly manipulative and it's ineffective on anybody with any grounded sense of self.

Likewise, with a narcissistic adult sibling, every conversation is a battle of wits which must have a winner or a loser? Are you always the loser, and by any means necessary? Do personal insults replace factual arguments, are they arguing the person instead of the principle? Do these so-called conversations deteriorate into a litany of personal and painful insults which have no relation to the subjects at hand? Do you always lose every argument? Only if you choose to compete, and then … you will lose. Because there's no winning an argument with a narcissist. It's best just to walk away … if they let you. Often a narcissist will refute a peaceful retreat with accusations of cowardice. Of course, the fear belongs to the narcissist, who is propelled by their very nature by insecurity and fear of abandonment and the destruction of their idealized self-image.

My brother is notorious for this. He takes irrational, insupportable stances and then holds them implacably. When he cannot argue he facts, he argues the man. He'll mock my expressive face, draw attention to my tendency to gesticulate (hand movements). Virtually any disagreement ends with a personal assault on me, relating not at all to the point in question. It's ugly, it's rude, it's reductive. And it's terribly narcissistic.

If your sibling won't take their portion of accountability for the conflict, that's a warning sign. Narcissists can't seem to do this, but the well-adjusted psyche can with little difficulty. This is a good warning sign of narcissism in just about any relationship. I've taken half the blame for my conflicts with my brother even though I don't deserve them. I don't force him to commit abuses. But as narcissist's are notoriously transactional, they cannot be made to feel that they alone are suffering or their outrage will be all the worse. So as a tactical position, it might be smart to deal with your own narcissistic adult siblings this way. It's a negotiation play, but it may placate them in times of conflict if you can't just walk away from them, which is generally best.

Favors as leverage is a good sign that you're being manipulated, and by a person who cares more (most) for their own benefit and little (none) for the other's. Though the shared transgression is presented at first as a bonding mechanism, it soon becomes a tool of empowered manipulation of one over the other. A narcissistic sibling will engage in a kind of schoolyard blackmail, leveraging other influential powers (physical threats as punishment) and offerings (extra dessert as reward) to lead the victimized sibling into a pattern of abuses which may easily continue through adulthood.

My brother did this to me recently, likely the last significant interaction of our adult lives. He invited me to rent a room in his house, temporarily, for a set price. He needed a little extra money, I needed a place to get my writing done while I was between domiciles. The proximity brought up old wounds, however, and his long-developing conditions had gotten worse. When the eventual outburst occurred, it was like an explosion of narcissism. For our purposes here, suffice it to say that he was quick to use the house as a weapon against me, as well as anything in it which I may have been using during my stay, including utilities (which had been included in the offer). The fact is that the narcissism will not offer anything without expecting something in return, probably something more … and then even more. For the narcissist, a relationship is a one-way street.

Sibling rivalry is a part of normal childhood balance, but it can come to an unhealthy point before most people, parents or children, are prepared to deal with it. Too much competition, which may be stoked by narcissistic parents, can create a dysfunctional sibling relationship.

The relationship between my brother and I share this classic narcissistic trait as well! I've never felt that I was in competition with him, as my career has been of the slower-developing type. Being a writer means years of sacrifice and toil, folks, and nobody pays you to teach yourself the craft.

But when I was last in close contact with my brother, I'd risen to greater heights in my own profession whereas he, sadly, had more or less fallen out of his own profession. This challenged him in a variety of narcissistic ways. It threatened his idealized self-image, it was transactionally disastrous for him. It stole from him one of his greatest manipulative tools (success) which, along with bartering favors, is a kind of financial abuse. He seethed with jealousy not only that I was gainfully employed and he was not, but that I was a writer, something he always had narcissistic fantasies about being, something he never quite achieved despite a few attempts.

Be aware of gaslighting and don't be taken in by it. Call it out! Chances are your narcissistic sibling will be so astounded by your insight that they won't know how to respond. They'll likely deny it or pretend they don't know what you're talking about. But that's just more lies, more manipulation, more gaslighting. My brother used sudden shifts in temperament to try to gaslight me.

If you're keen enough to clearly state your boundaries and your narcissistic sibling won't respect them, you've got a problem. Disrespect of clearly established boundaries is fundamentally lacking in empathy, and this is a hallmark of all abuses. Don't tolerate a violation of your boundaries, not by your siblings, your children, your lovers, your bosses, your coworkers, you friends; nobody.

Betrayals of confidence are a huge warning sign that you're dealing with a narcissist. This is so because narcissists don't care about anybody's confidences than their own. They see every bit of information as a weapon to be used when convenient. Never confide in a narcissist, no matter who they are. If you do, expect your confidence to be violated. The inherent difficulty here is that we are trained to trust family members above all, and as children (the most formative years) we really have no choice. But our choices as adults are different. We may face challenges, but equipped with the right information we have a chance to manage or simply refuse such behaviors. If you recognize these behaviors in yourself, you'll be particularly well-suited to countering them.

People-pleasing is something to look out for too. Narcissists often appeal to vanity, to insecurity, to anything which will help them to manipulate and control you. But they're not trying to please you, they're angling for you to please them. It's this selfish perspective which drives the narcissist, and it's something to be aware of, a serious red flag.

My brother did this, even to me. He can be charming and warm and hospitable, witty and welcoming. But these things are strategic for any narcissist, even more so for the sufferer of NPD.

The abusive behavior which accompanies narcissism is not to be tolerated. The narcissist will engage in any number of the abusive behaviors we've discussed, and all are dangerous to the victim in a variety of ways. The narcissist will make you feel that you deserve to be mistreated, and this is one of the greatest crimes a narcissist inflicts upon his or her children. Tolerance of abuse is one of the staples of a narcissist's success. Deny them that, and be aware when they take action to ensure it. Don't compromise on this. Don't back down. Give a narcissist an inch and they will take a mile, and in some situations this may mean taking your self-confidence, your self-actualization, and even your life.

You have to be your own advocate and be proactive about your own self-care. Yes, any narcissist will ridicule this. You may be called a snowflake (which, oddly are unique and magnificent and, when taken in great numbers, can bring down trees which weigh in the tons and can bring modern society to a screeching halt). Your feelings will be marginalized. My narcissistic brother did this to me, hurling insults of all types in a desperate attempt to break you down, replacing your self-respect with respect only for the narcissist. Do what I did and stand up for yourself …then get out. They talk about the fight-or-flight instinct. In this case, fight for yourself and then take flight, also for yourself.

You may want to think of this narcissistic sibling as a professional associate rather than as a family member. If you were a consultant, an accountant, a lawyer, and you had a client who was troublesome or unmanageable, you'd simply pull out of the professional relationship. So reframe things in your mind along those lines and it will make it easier to do what you have to do for your own wellbeing.

There will be times when avoidance is just not possible. You may have to collect with family for business purposes, inheritances as we discussed, making decisions about property and so on. In this case, if the relationship with a narcissistic sibling is especially troublesome, you might consider bringing a representative; a lawyer, perhaps an officer of the court. It will seem awkward, but it will be an effective way to prevent the almost inevitable conflicts which can arise from such a situation. Inheritances and family deaths will bring out the worst in the narcissistic sibling; entitlement, transactional thinking, unquestioning devotion; all are hallmarks of narcissism and all are titillated by large sums of family money or property to be divided. The narcissistic sibling may play along with equal division, but they will harbor resentment and feelings of victimization afterward. They'll resent you bringing in a third party, but they're going to resent everything anyway.

In my own experience, my brother was going to hire a man to scope out and control our sociopathic older brother at the middle brother's wedding. Eventually, the eldest (sociopathic) brother was simply left off the invitation list, while his ex-wife and child were welcomed. Sometimes, even a third party won't be enough.

Does your sibling always have to be the center of attention? Do they seem jealous when attention naturally falls on you? This may be familiar from your childhood, so look backward for the patterns. Think back to events which were dedicated to you; birthday parties, high school graduation, things of the sort. Was the narcissistic sibling there to celebrate you? Were they present at all? Did they ridicule the gifts you received, or even stole or destroyed them? This was an attempt to break down your sense of self, to which children are particularly vulnerable.

A narcissist has an exaggerated sense of self-importance and this can thus result in needing to be the center of attention. They can do this in many ways such as by monopolizing conversations, praising themselves, playing the victim, using illness or trying to get sympathy.

Narcissistic siblings, like all narcissists, need to be the center of attention, and often have superiority, rescue, and God complexes. So they may not stop at dressing down the victim sibling, their talents and gifts, but also their friends. A narcissist will use anything to manipulate the victim, and that includes friends. They will either degrade or marginalize them, or they will attempt to ruin the friendship or even steal it, anything at all to attack the victim's sense of self. Close friends are an appreciable part of anybody's sense of self, they're big contributors to a person's overall self-confidence and individuality, both things which are antithetical to the narcissist's successful manipulation.

My eldest brother doesn't need to be the center of attention necessarily, but he seethes with jealousy when I am. Meeting his friends, they showed an interest in me. But this only triggered my brother's sense of inadequacy.

I was in a rock band partnership with a good friend for most of my formative years. My narcissist older brother often tried to break up that friendship by implying I was joining other bands! Once I came home to the apartment I shared with this unnamed narcissistic older brother (actually a sociopath upon further investigation) and I found my two best friends sitting with my brother, and none of them welcomed me to join them. My brother had stolen my friends! And he did this for two reasons; his narcissism made making friends difficult for him. And he hoped to hurt me by transactionally taking my friends from me. If they were his friends, in his twisted mind, they couldn't be mine. In the short run this didn't work, and in the long run I'm not friends with any of them. But it's not the effect which is to be considered, but the motive and the actions.

Narcissistic siblings may assault your romances in the same way. For the same spiteful, transactional reasons, a narcissist cannot stand to see a sibling be happy or satisfied when they are not (or even when they are). They may undermine the romance by insinuating themselves into the romantic partner's company, introduce deconstructive dialogues, even seduce them without any real passion or desire. Their passion and desire is to build themselves up by breaking you down. Protect yourself and your relationships by keeping them as far away from you narcissistic siblings by any means necessary.

If you're succeeding in life, on whatever front, expect jealousy and even rage (as I was unfortunate enough to recieve). Because of the self-centered and transactional nature of narcissism, you sibling will not celebrate your successes but will seethe with jealousy over them. The more you succeed, the greater a failure they will be made to feel (by their own way of thinking). For your own protection, think about separating them from yourself, your friends, your intimate partners.

Envy is not only the enemy of a narcissist, but the closest ally. Because while envying others may undo the narcissistic sibling, the idea that others envy them is what helps them maintain their idealized self-image. Envy is what keeps them on top and in control. It's part of the unquestioning admiration they crave.

Like all narcissists, a sibling will show a distinct lack of empathy. If anything, they'll offer marginalization, disinterest, even ridicule. And they resent the empathy others may offer, since they feel it takes away from whatever empathy and attention the narcissistic sibling feels that they deserve instead. You probably notice that the transactional mindset is recurrent with narcissists, because it is.

Narcissistic siblings demonstrate the same sense of entitlement as other narcissists, but they use it in ways which are particular and exploitative of their siblinghood. They often feel that, as a sibling, they have greater rights to be abusive than those outside the family. This is not true nor is it to be tolerated. My sociopath brother did this to me, insulting me casually in a way he would do to nobody else. When I called him out on it, his answer was to wave me off and say, "Oh, you're my brother." This is not to be tolerated. A fluke of birth entitles nobody to anything.

Sibling rivalry is pretty common among siblings, and it may even be beneficial. It inspires kids to accept defeat, to strive toward achievement, to find and fulfill their hopes and dreams. But a narcissistic sibling will despise your achievements in that classically jealous, transactional fashion. They'll be exhibitionist and draw attention to themselves and compare your achievements to theirs, constantly hoping to establish their coveted superiority and preserve their idealized self-image. It's sad, really, but it's no less sad for the victim.

Like all narcissists, the narcissistic sibling will not accept responsibility or feedback, criticism or blame. They'll turn the blame on the victim sibling, they'll detract and deflect and use every ego-preserving technique to prevent facing criticism. My sociopath brother loves to dish it out, but he just can't take it. His favored technique is to ridicule progressive thought, assume the position of a sarcastic snowflake, and excuse himself as needing a safe space. It's a good way to be insulting while also being defensive. It's another example of the passive-aggressive tendencies of the narcissist.

The narcissistic sibling believes, like all narcissists, that they are entitled to better treatment, as they have often been given it. They feel that something makes them special, above and beyond judgement (as all narcissists do). But the narcissistic sibling will use this to make the victim sibling feel especially vulnerable to judgment in the same transactional way all narcissists see the world.

Another complication to having narcissistic siblings is that they likely learned those behaviors and traits from a narcissistic parent, as narcissism is a learned set of traits. Temperaments and natural personality traits and gifts may nurture or they may obstruct narcissistic tendencies, but narcissism and concurrent disorders are often learned and nurtured early in life. They develop through early adulthood and beyond, as we've seen.

To make matters worse, narcissistic parents are more apt to bond with narcissistic children than those which aren't narcissistic. Why is this? A number of reasons. The narcissistic parent sees themselves in their children and consider their children a reflection of their own greatness and achievement. They thrive on personality mirroring; they favor those who are most like them and so are supportive of their general worldview. So they gravitate to the children who are most like them, who exhibit the same narcissistic qualities. They also gravitate away from children, even their own, who are less like them (in other words, less narcissistic). They don't understand and cannot empathize with a contrary point of view to their own (another hallmark of narcissism) even when it comes from their own child. If you have you ever heard your own parents, or anyone else's, say something like, "I just don't understand that child," then you may know what this is all about.

Furthermore, this shared narcissism only confirms the natural state of the narcissism. I once knew a man who was given to screaming fits of rage. When asked (even when not) this particular grandiose narcissist (actually a sufferer of NPD) said simply, "My father screamed at me. We're a family of screamers." But those fits of rage are symptomatic of narcissism, as is the excusal of the abhorrent behavior.

The problem here (and it's a terrible problem) is that the victim child, basically the only well-adjusted person in this scenario, will inevitably be outnumbered. Narcissistic parents and likeminded children will stick together, they will share a marginalizing view of the victim sibling. The victim sibling is almost certain to perceive this. It's exclusionary treatment, which is a form of psychological abuse. When it happens to a kid from a parent (or a sibling) then it becomes child abuse. And when a victim sibling is the target of two or more narcissists in a single household, one from which there is no escape, the results can be devastating. The victim sibling/child may develop vulnerable narcissism, martyr and victim and guilt complexes, and more.

I felt outnumbered and hounded in the house of my stepfather and mother, which was dominated by a hardcore sociopath (my stepfather) and a developing narcissist well on his way through the cycle toward sociopathy himself. It was enough to drive me from my own mother's side, and that's not something any child does lightly.

And it may not be limited to a combination of one narcissist parent and one narcissist child. It's very likely that both parents will be narcissists and there could be several siblings who each have one variation of narcissism or another. A potentially well-adjusted child may have no chance but to fight fire with fire and adopt some form of narcissism just to survive.

It's hard to consider myself a narcissist, but I can identify some effects of my unfortunate rearing an essentially narcissistic household. They include insecurities and exhibitionism, if I'm being quite honest. All in all, I've been quite lucky not to have more signs of the condition.

So what does a victim sibling do when faced with a family of narcissists or even a single narcissistic family? The only healthy thing to do is get out, but this simply isn't feasible in almost every case. But imagine the poor child who scrambles to maintain his self-esteem and become self-actualized amid the negative and unbridled influences of a narcissistic household, where virtually every abuse is heaped upon them at different times, an unceasing barrage of abuses, often disguised as a twisted form of nurturing and parenting.

Pleased to meet you.

Luckily, I didn't succumb to the temptation of narcissism (I'm far too superior a person for that). But I recognize in myself traces of guilt complex, which is common among victims of family narcissism.

Dealing with a Narcissistic Sibling

If you can't cut off a narcissistic sibling (which may ultimately be best), you'll have to find ways of dealing with them. It won't be easy, but it's possible. Here are a few time-tested tips.

As we've said, it's pointless to argue with a narcissist, as they will not listen to reason. So the first thing you'll have to resist doing is telling them that they're narcissists, or trying to explain to them the sources or facts of their condition. The narcissist won't abide criticism, they have defensive mechanisms (deflection and projection) to reverse your intellectual approach. Are you a licensed psychoanalyst? That'll be the first thing they attack you on, to disqualify and marginalize you and your diagnosis, even if (especially if) you're right. Narcissists have amazing abilities to deny facts, and these are the first ones they'll deny as they cut to the heart of the narcissist's worldview. Don't waste your time and energy.

Trust yourself. Do not invest in anything a narcissistic sibling (or any narcissist) has to say.

Their opinions and judgments are objectively worthless, as they're so entirely subjective. Everything the narcissist sees comes through their distorted lens. The narcissist has a distorted self-image and also a distorted vision of the world; seeing the best in themselves and the worst in others. What we've established before holds true here; don't take it personally, because it's not about you.

Learn about NPD and narcissism, as you're doing now. Knowledge is power, and deliberate ignorance is a pillar of narcissism. You likely will not be able to help your narcissistic sibling, but you can help yourself. You're doing it right now! And once you've worked your way out of a toxic relationship with a narcissistic sibling, refer to our other books for insights into emotional intelligence, social skills, true leadership skills, and other essential skill sets.

It can be useful to get more knowledge about narcissism and on how to deal with it. It helps with accepting the situation and deciding how you want to move forward. You will learn it's not your fault and that you have the control and the power to decide your path from here.

Here's a handy checklist to keep in mind when identifying a narcissistic sibling:

- Is their company draining or sustaining?
- Is dialogue trying and confusing?
- Do they return to certain subjects which transgress your stated boundaries?
- Do they blame others, including you, for everything?
- Do they always compare (or avoid comparing) themselves to you, their accomplishments to yours?
- Do you trust them? Should you?

The hardest thing about dealing with a narcissistic sibling (or parent) is *not* dealing with them. But the terrible truth is that many narcissist can not only be untreatable but are certain to become worse with age. Childhood treatment, as we've seen, can develop into narcissism, which in time and without preventative treatment will develop into NPD. Toss in a little sadism, common among NPD sufferers, and the result is antisocial personality disorder, or sociopathy.

So, as painful and counter-instinctive as it may be, you may have to face the truth that the narcissist has to be let go, no matter who they are. Abandon your childhood hopes of winning their respect or admiration. Even if they harbor such feelings, the narcissistic sibling will be unable to express them. In fact, those feelings bring the narcissist terrible pain and confusion and almost always have to be denied or resisted.

If for some reason complete detachment isn't possible, consider emotional detachment. Be civil, tend to your family responsibilities, and leave it at that. Be as cursory and superficial as

If you must interact with such a sibling, be as emotionally distant as you can be; it will protect you and infuriate the narcissist. Be civil, answer questions, ask none. Don't bother explaining, don't ask for permission. Just do it; Nike that narcissist. Minimize contact too; only what is necessary and no more. Do not volunteer friendship, welcome, anything other than what is required by protocol and by law. Anything else will only open the door to more narcissistic abuses. You'll find the narcissist finds this frustrating, even insulting, a betrayal. Too bad. They see that in most things, but it's their problem.

But the modern family is more complicated than that, and so is the increasingly tangled web of narcissism and abuse which goes along with it. To further untangle it, we move from blood relatives to stepfamily, the source of extraordinary conflict and abuses, even today.

CHAPTER SIX: Narcissistic Stepparents and Stepsiblings

From Cain and Abel to *Cinderella*, we know look at stepmothers and their counterparts. Though a fairy tale, there are truths in that ages-old tale. Stepparent relationships face real challenges which can originate with both nature and nurture, and an increasingly common relationship as well. This, sadly, means that the attendant abuses are also becoming more common. With the rate of divorce skyrocketing worldwide, the cases of stepparenting situations is steadily on the rise.

The best available information tells that, as recently as 2020, the United Kingdom was continuing to see a rise in divorce rates. Requests for divorce in Australia increased a tragic 200% that year. Divorce filings in Turkey increased 400%. In the US, roughly 45% of first marriages ended in divorce, 60% of second marriages, and 73% of third marriages.

The United States Bureau of Census reports that over 50% of families are re-coupled or remarried, creating roughly 1,300 new stepfamilies every day.

So let's take a look at narcissism in this relationship, on the part of the stepparent and the stepchild as well. Then, we'll turn our attention to narcissism in stepsiblings, also an ongoing problem in modern domestic life.

When discussing stepparents, it's very often the stepmother who comes to mind. From Cinderella's fairy tale tormentor onward, the stepmother is often villainized, and that's a shame. Very often, any stepparent gives their all to raise a child who is not even their own. It's too common for them to be rejected by the stepchild, who may bring up the inarguable fact that the stepparent is not their real parent. And while this is true, there's little arguing that the stepparent does (or should be by most laws) perform the function of the parental role in question. A stepmother is still a mother figure, just as a stepfather is a father figure in the household, regardless of biological concerns.

There are also a great many successful stepparenting relationships. My own grandfather was a stepfather (my birth grandfather, reportedly a member of the infamous gangster group the Purple Gang, abandoned my mother and grandmother to start another family). But I knew only one man to be my grandfather, and he was a dutiful and likable patriarch. This is not necessarily a toxic relationship.

Then, of course, there were the instances of my stepmother and stepfather. More about them in a short while.

What happens when the stepparent is (as mine both were) a narcissist?

A narcissistic stepmother can cause all manner of psychological stress and emotional chaos in an already-fractured family. This is so because stepmothers are uniquely positioned to manipulate both their husbands and their husband's children. A stepmother, like any woman, has a biological mandate to reproduce. They have limited years when this is physically possible (unlike their husbands). So they have biological reasons to marginalize another woman's children.

Another facet unique to stepmothers may raise some progressive feathers. But put away your presumptions and read on. Men and women all over the world have certain roles they play in society. The roles vary, and many times one person performs several functions (a woman may be a wife, a mother, a workplace teammate, a lover, a friend) often several of them at once. That's perfectly normal and well and proper. But there are still traditional aspects to these roles. Until this generation and to some degree the generation before it, the roles were more strictly drawn. This is still true to a great extent today. Men comprise the majority of the armed forces in most Western countries. They dominate the United States workforce and are notoriously paid more for it.

These traditional roles often put the wife at home. True, in 2021 she may be working from home, so too may be her husband. But the traditional role of the mother figure as homemaker is still very much at play, at least psychologically. Even the term stay-at-home mom only exists because of the new and generationally unusual concept of the working mom. It's more common, but tradition still looms large in the psyche.

A mother is biologically different than a father; they provide different elements to a child's education. Women breastfeed, men do not. Women are often more open and giving with their emotions than their male counterparts. The female human vocal chords are fundamentally different than a human males, encompassing an entirely different register. Women are often not physically capable of communicating with the same timbre than men. Dogs recognize this, and for this reason they are less obedient to female owners than male owners (this is so because the human male's voice is more like a dog's, so the dog understands it on a primitive level more clearly than a female's voice).

The biological and cultural aspects goes deeper. Due to these traditional preconceptions, boys are often raised to fulfill their roles (outward projections of strength) and girls to fulfill their own roles (outward projections of sexuality). It sounds unfair and it is. But young women learn to wear cosmetics, most young men don't. Why is this? Women are sadly locked into certain traditional roles and they're often indoctrinated in the ways of performing those roles. For generations, women have been marginalized in society. Their only chance for participation to any degree meant exploiting their strengths. Instead of being stronger, they had to be cagier, smarter. Even today, a woman has to be twice as clever as a man to get half as far.

And this is the real strength when dealing with children, who are at a natural disadvantage intellectually. They're certainly at a disadvantage in dealing with a narcissist, much less when the narcissist is their mother figure, whom they need to trust. That trust is the key to effective manipulation, which we know is the narcissist's stock in trade.

What does all this mean? Women are often positioned to spend more time with the children of the house. They are expected by instinct and ingraining to be nurturing and loving. Children rely upon them for this, as if hardwired to do so.

Now consider the child whose birthmother is absent. She may be divorced, she may be dead. But this creates a real wanting in the heart of the child. Children in almost any species (all mammals and birds) are hardwired to seek out the nurturing and protection of their mothers. Mothers are genetically hardwired to protect them, as they must invest so much in gestation. But that's parenting by birth. In point of fact, stepparenting rarely happens in nature. Lions are known for killing the offspring of their predecessors in order to establish their own genetic dominance. Elephants raise their young as a community, not as a lone couple, as do orca.

But we humans have created and popularized divorce, and so created the stepparent. Now let's put a narcissist in the role of a stepmother and see what happens: They are uniquely close to the children and to their father, her husband. She can manipulate both with incredible effectiveness. As the children are trained to obey their mother figure and seek her love and acceptance, the narcissist will get just what they want and need. The child's natural yearning for a mother figure make them particularly susceptible to this kind of manipulation. Narcissists are naturally manipulative and this puts them in a perfect position to indulge those inclinations. They can also exploit the needs of a man who, for whatever reason, has lost his wife. She may use sexual abuse tactics (withholding sex or using it as a reward) to manipulate her husband. She may lie about her intentions (narcissists are never forthcoming, as they fear the truth being used against them).

Stepmothers have every advantage that a narcissistic birthmother has, but she has more reason to exploit it. The stepmother has no biological attachment to the children and often craves a biological attachment to her own unborn children. But unlike a lion, she can't just kill the previous offspring. So she has reason to break them down, to make them doubt themselves. An adversarial relationship is common here. As children grow, they discover their own identities, and this is antithetical to the narcissist's sense of control, as we've already seen.

Remember that a stepmother may feel that she is in competition with the children over control over the patriarch. A father, especially one separated from the children's birthmother, will often have a sense of guilt and additional responsibility to care for his motherless children. This makes him vulnerable to exploitation by the children. The stepmother knows this, and may feel she has to compete to better the child's efforts. But remember that what is narcissistic in adults is merely a survival instinct in children. Remember also that children lack the intellectual acumen which adults have and which adult narcissists use so adroitly. This gives the stepparent a distinct advantage, the stepmother especially.

What's sad and sick is when the stepmother, a narcissist, has an agenda to deliberately isolate the children from their father (a way to control both parties) and each other in the case of siblings (control of the children). It's particularly easy for the narcissist and they are positioned by tradition and often by practicality to inflict the damage which the narcissist does so well.

The narcissistic stepmother has an additional advantage; the absence of the mother. She can them be marginalized or villainized to further confuse the children. Remember that the narcissist has no empathy, and they may even have a sadistic element to their personalities. In this case, the narcissistic stepmother may inflict terrible damage on the children and even enjoy doing so.

There's another tradition-based aspect which is intrinsic to the role of stepmother. In the United States, women are notoriously paid less than men (roughly 80% of men in an equal job, and that happens outside the US too). This may give many women a unique financial interest in securing her place in a family which she did not create. A woman may marry for money, and so may a man. But the inequity in wages according to gender means a woman, any woman, has a greater financial strain than a man. That's just the sad fact. If you don't like it, change it (don't shoot the messenger). At the very least, you owe it to yourself and those you love to understand it.

There's another aspect to consider, and that's the stepmother's competition with the absent mother. While competition is common in adults of both genders, they compete on generally different fields. This draws us back to traditional roles, undeniable even in our progressive society. Men compete in terms of erectile function, income, bodily size and strength. Women compete in terms of beauty and utility. Beauty is emphasized in our modern Western world, particularly for women. Youth also plays a part in the role of the stepmother while it may be irrelevant to the male counterpart because of biological circumstances we've already discussed. The stepmother finds herself having to be younger and more beautiful than her predecessor, which she often may be, considerations a father may simply not have. Women have things to offer which are unique to her position in the household, and that's more children. This may appeal to the father's natural instincts to procreate. But it only complicates relations with the stepchild or stepchildren. Any person is likely to favor their own natural-born children over the stepchildren of some other woman. It's a longstanding tradition which has darkened my own childhood, as I'll discuss shortly.

Financial considerations may arise again as age makes a narcissistic stepmother even more reliant on family money. Man or woman, agism in the Western world is a stone-cold fact. A woman of a certain age is even more certain to be discriminated against. That means their needs and reliance is greater. A stepmother cannot afford and will likely not abide contests from adult children for control of a late patriarch's estate. It can be a legally complicated matter, one which often favors the spouse over the children. But any woman in this position will be preparing for the future, their future foremost. If they have children of their own, their interest will be even greater. So it's easy to see that a narcissistic stepmother will be preparing for this in advance. If there are two stepchildren, she may turn on against the other in a divide-and-conquer strategy. She may turn the father against his own children, using the absentee mother as a device in her manipulation. When preparing for her own future or the future of her biological children, the narcissistic stepmother may do almost anything.

Stepchildren of such a woman will have little recourse but to steady on. Knowledge is power. There's little advantage in a challenge, as children have the disadvantage in such a conflict in virtually every case. Once adults, the children may disengage emotionally or use any of the devices we've looked at so far. The woman is your father's spouse, not your own. If officers of the court are required to preserve financial interests, use them.

What's particularly egregious about a narcissistic stepmother is that more participation is required in child-rearing. Traditional roles often put the stepmother in closer contact with the stepchild. It gives her as much time and proximity as she needs to do her narcissistic works. Neglect is often part of this, detaching from a stepchild once their utility is no longer as great. A stepmother may, for example, promise new motherhood for the child in order to secure their would-be husband's trust. Once the marriage contract is signed, the bogus offers of friendship and motherhood may be retracted. But the vulnerable child, more than the intellectually superior father, believes the promises and is even more damaged by that betrayal. The father still gets what he was promised, after all. Only the child is denied, neglected, and in so doing is abused.

The tendency for narcissistic stepparents, stepmothers especially, is to be erratic and blameful. My own stepmother would be triggered by the slightest resistance into fits of rage. True, she had issues having to replace another woman, but she was also a narcissist; radically insecure and in desperate need of constant obedience, unable to externalize or empathize.

A stepparent has a certain otherness which children understand. They are also thrust into the role of authority in the household, as we've discussed. When they explode into a rage, it has an alien feel to the child, an assaultive effect which is particularly frightening. Why? Because instinct tells the child that (in a perfect world) their parent will not harm them. It's a biological imperative that they don't. But a stepparent lacks that biological ingredient and children know that. In conflict, the child lacks the innate reassurance of safety when dealing with a stepparent, especially a narcissistic stepmother.

My own stepmother, Nancy, was several cases in point. Her narcissistic personality disorder manifested itself in a variety of ways. Once again it's notable that not all the behaviors present in a single case, as that is rare.

I can't say Nancy had an exaggerated sense of self-importance, but she did require excessive admiration from her friends. She lorded her early-life achievements as more impressive than they were as a symptom of her insecurity having married a much more successful man. She may not have been preoccupied with fantasies of perfection, but she did have a snobbery and superiority which I believe even her friends perceived. She was certainly given to looking down on others, including her own friends and, strangely, the children of her friends. Perhaps it's better to say she liked to compare her own child to her children's friends. I don't know how many times she'd say something to Danielle like, "You don't want to be like Debra, do you?"

Nancy was gracious enough not to dominate conversations, nor was she particularly exploitative. But there is a story which is telling of her narcissism.

Our parents had an acrimonious divorce, followed by years of custody battles. At one point my father decided against the bargain of a child for a wife and he broke it off with Nancy, telling her to find a man who would be the husband and father she wanted.

But Nancy wasn't convinced. She began turning up at my mother's house, where she lived with her husband, Willard, and their daughter Robin. She still wanted to visit with me and my brothers, taking us to the movies and so on. It was very confusing for three young minds and hearts already thrown into a prolonged and chaotic familial state.

After a few weeks, Nancy's plan worked (somehow) and my father proposed. Nancy clearly had not so valued the friendship or company of three pre-teen boys or their mother and stepfather. She used us boys as a way of getting the husband she wanted. And, sad as it is to say, she used her husband to get the daughter she wanted. To be fair, my father got the wife he wanted.

Nancy did not exhibit the narcissist's unwillingness or inability to empathize, and she didn't evince much envy either. She did have the narcissist's haughty manner, however, and was given to great shows of pretense. She rarely overlooked a chance to refer to her history in New York, one of the world's great cities (though her family was from Queens).

Nancy did want the best of everything, as many narcissists do. She needed a car phone when they were still a luxury (what? I'm old), a diesel luxury car when those were in fashion, things of the sort.

And, like a lot of narcissists, Nancy could be quick to anger at a whiff of criticism. She was given to the quick-tempered outbursts of unwarranted rage and moodiness of a narcissist.

Of the popular abuses, Nancy was prone to verbal and psychological of a covert nature. She was given to backhanded compliments (insults disguised as compliments) and marginalization. Her complexes included superiority and martyr. She was given to acts of identity abuse, one story rings in my memory.

I think I was about ten years old. Nancy had planned a day at the park with me and my sister, Danielle. At the last minute, I opted out. I suppose playing with a four-year-old just wasn't appealing to my ten-year-old self. I realize, in retrospect, that I'd given my word and was trying to renege on it.

Teaching a child to keep their word is surely a good thing. Admittedly, I spent a lot of time indoors and a bit of sunshine and exercise could only be healthy for a growing boy.

But the truth is that she was counting on me to entertain my sister so she could talk to her friends. There might have been an element, also, of her pride. She didn't like being denied, especially not by me. I think she didn't like the idea of showing up to her friends without having wrangled control over me, to appear weak to them.

Whatever her motivation, when I denied her, Nancy exploded into a rage, for which I was totally unprepared. Instead of calmly explaining the benefits of going despite my changing whims, instead of being honest, she took a different route.

She dressed me down as selfish, a parasite, on the take (a phrase she used). She told our maid at the time to deny me anything and everything (showing no empathy for the maid and demonstrating willful neglect and bartering necessities against unquestioned obedience). I remember at the time reflecting to a time not long before when she and my father reassured me it was my house, where I belonged. Suddenly, I was on the take. I wish I knew then not to take it as personally as I did.

In the end, I went to the park, Nancy maintained the control she needed, and life went on. But the experience is a good case in point on narcissistic stepparents. Nancy would never have said that to her own birth-daughter, Danielle.

Now, to be fair, we turn our attention to the equally unique position of the narcissistic stepfather.

The traditions we've discussed, still very much at play in our modern society. As such, a stepfather is more likely to be out of the house working (or working in the house, but still working). A narcissistic father has power over stepchildren which even a stepmother doesn't have.

Physiologically speaking, we know the vocal chords of the human male and the human female are different. The human male has a much lower register. This gives them a frightening sense of command which can terrify a child. And since a stepfather lacks the biological bond, he may be more apt to holler at stepchildren than his own natural-born children. A stepparent may also be given to physical abuses and even sexual abuses. Studies indicate that stepchildren are five times more likely to suffer abuses in the home than birthchildren, including sexual abuse.

The same complications which make a stepparent threatening to a child apply to stepfathers as much as stepmothers. Not only do they lack the natural attachment of blood relatives, they may feel the natural compulsion to destroy the offspring of the previous husband and father. Lions do this, and there's a very real, natural reason for this. For the stepfather of almost any species, room has to be made for their own progeny.

And, like a stepmother, a stepfather may feel an unnatural sense of competition with the person they're replacing. A stepfather's pride and sense of manhood could be threatened by this previous parent. But it's hard to compete with the idealized image of an absent parent. For whatever reason, they're not around to participate in the daily challenges of child-rearing. It leaves the stepparent to make all the mistakes, while the absent parent gets all the glory. This can be frustrating for any stepparent, but for a stepfather even more so. A lot of a man's sense of self-respect comes from a sense of control in the household. A stepfather may have to go to greater lengths to assert this control, a narcissistic stepfather even more so.

A stepfather also has what a stepmother may lack; upper body strength. This can be used to intimidate, even terrorize, stepchildren. Again, there's no natural reassurance that the child won't be physically harmed. In fact, there is the natural compulsion to generate harm to the child. A child can sense this even if they cannot understand it.

Any stepparent may feel a sense of competition with the man he replaced. The narcissistic stepfather is especially susceptible to this. And as the traditions we mentioned change along with economic shifts, it's increasingly common that the stepfather may not be working. This can threaten the man's sense of his own manhood, especially if the previous father did or continues to work. It's a matter of pride, which is more emotional than rational. Unfortunately, emotional reactions (rather than rational responses) can often be aggressive or even violent. A narcissist who is denied the adoration and ceaseless respect they need can resort to outward expressions of their frustration. Substance abuse may be common, and this can only lead to greater, concurrent abuses; physical, mental, and sexual.

This lends another complication to the tale of the narcissistic stepfather. Because while it's extremely rare for a stepmother to commit acts of sexual abuse against stepchildren of either gender, the narcissistic stepfather may become sexually abusive of a stepdaughter. There's no biological connection to prevent this abuse, as there is between blood relatives (even this is not always sufficient to prevent sexual abuses, sadly). And a frustrated stepfather, lacking in self-esteem and resentful of the man he is replacing, intoxicated and angry with a teenage girl who is not his blood relative, may lash out in any number of terrible ways we've already examined.

Remember that we're not talking about stepfathers as a group, but the case of narcissistic stepfathers. It's the narcissism which allows the self-idealized narcissist to believe they have rights which others don't have, that they should be able to do as they please without ramifications. In the service of their own sense of justice, the narcissistic stepfather may rationalize almost anything.

Complicating matters is that the father, a child's natural protector, isn't around to protect them. It is a biological compulsion to protect one's offspring, but the stepparent of either gender lacks this natural compulsion. In fact, they may be fighting the opposite compulsion, to destroy the offspring, even if they don't realize it.

So the narcissistic and abusive stepparent may not even realize that they're being abusive to the stepchild. On the other hand, we know that narcissists are almost always aware of what they're doing, unlike sufferers of narcissistic personality disorder.

A big part of narcissism is rage. The narcissist is given to explosions of temper, and when this comes from an unrelated parent to a frightened child, the effects can be devastating. Children may live in terror, be driven to guilt and victim complexes, vulnerable narcissism, and other debilitating conditions.

Worse, the narcissistic stepfather is likely to hand down this narcissism to the child, who may replicate the abusive behavior despite their own compulsion to rebel against the stepparent. This rebellion is bound to be seen by the narcissistic stepfather as a betrayal, a refusal of their authority. This will incite further rage responses, greater frustration, denial of the narcissistic needs; this can create a downward spiral of resentment, alienation, and estrangement.

And, like the narcissistic stepmother, the narcissistic stepfather is charismatic. He may charm the stepchild to disarm their defenses. He may turn one child against another. He may try to convince the stepchild that their birth father is somehow unworthy. And all this may occur under the pretense of love and supportive child-rearing. Or the narcissistic stepfather (and stepmother) may be passive-aggressive, ridiculing the absent parent, using back-handed compliments, and otherwise undermining the replaced parent in the mind and heart of the child. This is how a narcissistic stepfather may manipulate the stepchild, creating doubt and a lack of self-assurance and self-confidence.

The narcissistic stepfather has another cruel trick up his sleeve. The narcissist, you'll remember, must be superior to others. This sense of superiority is primary to their psychological construct and it's easily threatened, even by a child's love for their absent birth father. But instead of being frank about this, the narcissistic stepfather may level constant criticism, deny praise as a reward or even support. They will rationalize this as good parenting, but really it's just psychological abuse, a way to break down the child's sense of self-worth.

This brings us to the unpleasant example of my own narcissistic stepfather. Actually, as he had a severely sadistic bent, I'd diagnose him as antisocial personality disorder. So … this should be fun.

Willard's early successes gave him an exaggerated self-importance, key to his narcissism and his disorder. He required excessive admiration and, refused it, reacted swiftly and sternly. He would not be contradicted. He would claim that he was teaching respect, in the old-fashioned ways of his own upbringing. But in point of fact he was radically insecure, another facet of narcissism.

Willard had a superiority complex and a rescue complex, positioning himself as the key player in his household. He would not let my mother work, for example, as it threatened his sense of control over the household, another hallmark of the narcissist. The constant custody battles threatened that same sense of control and superiority, appealing to his insecurity. He was preoccupied with visions of his own success, and these visions took him from one desperate bid for success after another. The sum total of his efforts were that my mother became the breadwinner of the family, an even greater threat to his control and sense of masculinity.

He could be quite charming, in the way of the narcissist, with good comic timing and an almost encyclopedic knowledge of good punchlines.

Willard also had little to no empathy, at least not for me. The only phone call I ever received from him was the day my kid sister died. He said, "Your sister's taken a turn for the worse."

I asked, "How bad?"

He answered, "The worst." And we never spoke of it again.

He felt directly competitive with our father, who loomed large in his absence. He was envious of my father's superior accomplishments, I believe. He was verbally abusive of my father, and so was psychologically abusive of us.

He tended to monopolize conversations at the dinner table, belittling anybody and everybody.

Not that he wasn't funny, until he got too drunk. And he drove around in fancy jaguars which he couldn't afford, a pretense to his fading wealth and dwindling prospects.

When contradicted he was erratic and rageful, given to histrionics. He was vulnerable to stress and failed to adapt to change or to regulate his behavior, causing the end of his career. Afterward, he fell into a deep depression, also a hallmark of narcissism. And I know for a fact that he harbored feelings of guilt, vulnerability, shame, and humiliation, though he never would have admitted this.

His abuses included substance (the cause of his premature death), verbal and psychological. His complexes included martyr, superiority, and hero.

But let's get back to the feelings of vulnerability, shame, guilt, and humiliation. There were various reasons for this, from guilt associated with his daughter's head injury, to even more deeply rooted problems. As this chapter is about narcissistic stepparents, we'll stick with that and I'll share a story which you may find interesting, unique, and particular to this subject.

It turns out that my stepfather himself had endured a peculiar episode as a kid, one I only learned about from a blood relative of his years later. We'd all assumed he was born to his parents and raised in a traditional manner. His parents were reliable and respected, his father was a judge.

But it turns out that his mother had something like what we'd now call post-partum depression, perhaps a kind of panic attack. The infant Willard was handed over to another woman to raise, and he fell in love with her new charge. Not long afterward (long enough, it seems) Willard's mother had a change of heart and, in accordance with the laws at that time, retrieved the child. Willard's birth parents raised him, while his brokenhearted (and fleeting) foster parent committed suicide.

Of course, this is not the fault of the young Willard. I don't know that he harbored guilt over it (I don't know what feelings he harbored about it or most other things). But it's easy to see his perception of the recurrent pattern. As a child, he'd created an attachment to a non-parent guardian and that attachment proved fatal. I'm not saying that he felt his love for me would push him to suicide (on the contrary), but it's clear how he could see that any emotional investment in another person's son could be dangerous, be misspent. So for him to cut me off when I left his household (and he remained emotionally detached from me for the rest of his life, increasingly so) at least hindsight can give us some insight into the workings of his mind and heart.

I don't think anything excuses a grown man from making war on a little boy for the crime of loving his father, but it does go to show that these things can be complex and reliant on any number of chaotic external factors.

Dealing with a Narcissistic Stepparent

Stepchildren are generally innocent of any real wrongdoing in such a relationship. True, children may act out from a sense of loss, and children naturally exhibit more narcissistic tendencies and behaviors by virtue of their youth, as we've already seen. The abuses of a stepparent can undermine a child's sense of worth (which is often the intention of the narcissistic stepparent) and may last a lifetime.

If the replaced parent, birth mother or father, is still alive and available to the child, that relationship should be encouraged and nurtured. The stepparent will object, but legal precedent does allow parents access to their children, with few exceptions. The laws in the United States generally do grant custody to the mothers, however, which means the greater likelihood is that the father will be the absent parent. Unfortunate statistics in urban areas means a child may be unlikely to have access to a possibly incarcerated parent.

Siblings of a narcissistic stepparent should be encouraged to strengthen that relationship. Siblings in this situation may be the only people the other can trust. It's unfortunate that the narcissistic stepparent of either gender may try to split the children and turn them against each other. The reasons should be clear; it's the strength of their blood bond which may threaten the control the stepparent needs to feel secure. So siblings should cling to one another and remain vigilant against any efforts to turn one against the other. When there are several children, this is even more important. When one child is turned against the other, it's bad. But when two children are turned against a single, third child (often the youngest) the results can be cruel and devastating. The youngest child may develop inferiority and victim complexes, among other things.

The children are innocent by virtue of their age. But children can still react emotionally, which they're likely to do in the absence of a birth parent. It's natural for a child, though not always pleasant. It's unnatural for a child to be separated from their birth parent, and it can be difficult for the child to deal with it. Being in the company of an unrelated narcissist is itself a challenge. When combined, children may be pushed to unreasonable emotional reactions.

Most parents would be sympathetic and supportive, as this is the biological imperative which blood parents have and which stepparents lack. The narcissistic parent cannot externalize the child from their behavior and they cannot resist taking it personally. So a maturing child may be made aware that they're triggering their narcissistic stepparent's behavior. Even a child may be able to calibrate their behavior in ways that a narcissistic adult of either gender cannot.

All this emotional overload may just make a child retract as a matter of self-care. They can tune out, as it were, and never tune back in. This can create a lifetime of isolation and depression.

What's most unfortunate is that the stepchild's actual present birthparent, father or mother, may be enthrall to the charms and manipulation of the stepparent. This makes them ineffectual in protecting the children from these devious abuses. They may be too ready to accept the tough-love approach of their new spouse. Narcissists manipulate everyone around them, never forget that.

As is the case with most narcissists, virtually anyone with NPD, and all sociopaths, the best relationship is no relationship at all. Once eighteen and out of the house (in some cases before this if granted by a court of law) a stepchild of a narcissistic stepparent should consider simply cutting them off. Unfortunately, it's more than likely that the stepparent will already be splitting the spouse from their birth children. So cutting off the narcissistic stepparent may mean limiting access to the birth parent, and this can be a crushing blow, one the narcissist in question probably well understands. They're likely to use access to the birth parent as a weapon against the adult stepchild. Remember that the stepchild may have lost their absent birth parent to death or incarceration, so to lose the only other birth parent they have can be terrible, almost insufferable. The clever, calculating narcissistic stepparent knows this. They know also that their spouse will have the same challenges in being estranged from their birth children. But the step may have created children between the two, and these birth children are perfectly positioned to satisfy the spouse's biological parental impulses and instincts, making it easier to distance them from the children of a previous marriage.

Narcissistic Stepchildren

It's a sad fact that narcissism is a learned collection of traits encouraged by a person's natural temperament and handed down by adult narcissists. This is no different in the case of stepparenting relationships. Even in the midst of conflict, the child is apt to reflect the behavior of the parent or stepparent. That means abusive stepparents are likely to raise abusive children, and narcissistic parents are likely to pass along their tendencies to children in the household. Since true narcissism is best identified in adults (children exhibit signs of narcissism which are natural in their underdeveloped psyches), this may not evince until the stepchild has reached or is nearing adulthood.

The fault of this development must lay with the parent or stepparent, but what can be done about it? If you're in this situation, chances are your own narcissistic tendencies influenced your child, or your caught between a narcissistic spouse and a narcissistic teen or adult child.

In this case, you can take steps. First, contribute as much positive energy as you can. Narcissists are transactional by nature, so be careful not to praise one and not the other. What the narcissist craves is inequality, so counter it with equality. It's another case of denying the narcissists what they crave, of not playing into their game or enabling their complexes or disorders.

Show them both compassion and empathy. Narcissists lack empathy, and they have little understanding of it. Show them both equal empathy, and they will be stymied. True, they'll likely find some narcissistic behavior to counter this, blaming you and finding fault with your efforts. Let them, they're only fighting against themselves and that just may lead them to some illumination or enlightenment.

The situation can be trying for the parent caught between two narcissists. They value the love of both, they're likely eager to share their love with both. But when the two are at odds, and are coming at one another from narcissistic viewpoints, the only psychologically sound member of the family is caught between them. In this case, self-care is what counts. The embattled spouse/parent can suffer considerably in these circumstances, with feelings of guilt and shame. It's easy for this parent to feel they let their children down, failed in a primitive and biological way. Otherwise or in addition thereto, they may feel that they've failed as a spouse to the frustrated narcissistic stepparent. Sadly, this plays into the narcissist's hands. The narcissistic child and spouse will both manipulate the innocent parent/spouse, using their love for the other as a means to manipulate them. With divided loyalties and the stress which goes along with it, the parent caught in the middle may suffer from subsequent conditions like depression, doubt, and may resort to substance abuse and suffer poor sleep cycles, poor health, premature death, and even suicide.

These conflicts between implacable narcissistic stepparents and stepchildren may even destroy the second marriage. When one narcissist permanently disengages from the other, as is often recommended, the innocent parent/spouse may be put in a position of having to choose between the two. But spouses serve a different function in an adult's life than their children. There is a natural and social mandate which requires some separation of parents and children. Adult children are meant to leave the house, to find their own spouses and have their own children. True, our society maintains intergenerational bonds, also a good and healthy thing. Spouses, especially second spouses, are not naturally poised to leave the house. The whole point of marrying a second time is to stay married, for one not to leave the other. Also, as we get older, finding a good companion gets more and more difficult. Think about it; an eligible single man or woman in their twenties has more biological value than either one in their forties. And nobody wants to die alone. All this means the embattled parent/spouse is more apt to side with their spouse over their own blood child or children. The narcissistic spouse/parent knows this and, manipulative as they are, they're likely to use it to their advantage.

The narcissistic child is no better. They will manipulate the parent, possibly regressing to appeal to their instincts.

A person in this situation is well-advised to stay out of it. Resist attempts at split, show equal love to both. Separate the relationships and the relations, if need be. See each narcissist on their own, deal with these relationships on a one-on-one basis. And be aware of the risks to your own self-care.

For me? My stepmother died suddenly and my stepfather died slowly, so there was little time or purpose to resolving the conflicts. What was past was past, I was on my own, fate would play its hand as it always does. Pity, though, as I would relish the opportunity to speak to either one, for my own sake if not for theirs.

Our look at narcissism in families continues, stretching out from the core of parents and their children, between blood-siblings to stepparents and their children. (Narcissism between step-children is easier to avoid in adulthood, as a clean cut is easier to accomplish. Otherwise, the same techniques may apply.) So the tendrils of our scrutiny continue to stretch outward further, to grandparents. They are the family members who occupy the next layer of intimacy, and they may also be vulnerable to narcissistic abuses in both directions, as we'll soon see.

CHAPTER SEVEN: Narcissistic Grandparents and Grandchildren

It only makes sense that narcissism would be pervasive in the senior community. Though we know that symptoms may abate with time, we also know that narcissism is a progressive and corrosive state. It's only likely to get worse with time, and that's one thing seniors have over their younger counterparts; they've had more time to let their progressive narcissism get worse and worse.

Why? Consider the elements of narcissism: lack of empathy, insecurity, need for unquestioned adoration and obedience, hyper-sensitivity to criticism. Now think of the life of any average senior in the United States or other Western countries: treated without empathy, often made financially and biologically (or medically) insecure, deprived of adoration or even attention, no longer able to command obedience, the target of criticism. It's only natural that those with narcissistic tendencies would exploit all of these conditions. And if they're narcissists, they're likely to be at the advanced states, making these adaptations all the more likely.

The aged's greater needs make these narcissistic behaviors more necessary to survival, as in the case with children. But seniors have what children lack; self-regulation and self-awareness. Even more keenly aware of what they're doing and why, the senior narcissist also has the advantage of being what all narcissists crave; automatic forgiveness. Let's face it; a senior can say virtually anything and get away with it.

Let's take a minute to note that the aged are susceptible to all manner of physiological brain malfunction, such as Parkinson's or Altzhiemer's, which may account for legitimate delirium. More often than not, however, it's a simple matter of narcissism. The aged narcissist knows whatever they say may be attributed to bygone social standards or dementia. A narcissistic senior may even feign delirium as an excuse to behave in an antisocial manner. This is something neither the narcissistic child nor parent can get away with. Racism, outbursts of rage and temper; the senior can justify any kind of behavior.

And while they were developing that lifetime's worth of narcissism or NPD, they are likely to be developing complexes which are common to narcissism and the elderly; a potent combination. The elderly may easily develop exaggerated martyr and victim complexes, which inflicts terrible guilt on adult children and grandchildren.

Seniors are unlikely to develop abusive behaviors like physical, sexual, or substance abuses, especially if they live in controlled environments. Living on their own, abuse of alcohol and even prescription medication remains likely among the elderly. The mix of alcohol and prescription medication can create another set of antisocial behaviors, so this should be the focus of anybody who believes their elder parent or grandparent may be a narcissist.

Assuming no undue influence from medicinal interaction, seniors are likely to slip into other abuses, particularly verbal, psychological, and identity abuses. As they can say just about anything and get away with it, a narcissistic senior is likely to say anything to anyone, no matter how cruel and inappropriate. These narcissistic seniors used to be narcissistic parents, after all, and were probably raised by narcissistic parents, as we've seen. They've had a lifetime of manipulation to perfect their techniques, and as seniors they're given *carte blanche* to execute their strategies.

They're also given all manner of opportunities. Seniors are marginalized in society, that's hard to dispute. And that gives them reason to complain, to criticize, to control.

But what is special about the relationship between the narcissistic senior and their grandchild? It's the gap of a single generation, which is a greater distance between the two than merely thirty years or so.

As we've seen, any parent has a biological connection to their children; it's a natural mandate. Were this not so, mass cannibalization would wipe out life on Earth. It's often speculated, in fact, that the reason young mammals are so cute (big eyes, small noses) is to prevent their parents from killing and eating them. It's also said that there's no greater love than that of a mother for her child, nor any greater loss than that of a child to a suffering mother. And when that mother becomes a grandmother, the bond between her and the grandchild will naturally be less strong, less intimate. The grandmother didn't carry the grandchild the way she did her own child, after all. The grandmother (in most circumstances) doesn't spend countless hours of every day and night tending to the infant, often nursing them with their own breast milk.

In point of fact, the bonds between grandchildren and grandparents seems to be becoming weaker as society progresses. Humans were more clannish in the earliest years of recorded history and even before. Paleolithic man had survival needs which modern man does not have. Originally, we were part of the natural food chain, predators and prey like every other living creature. But domestication and socialization took the human being out of the food chain, for all intents and purposes. Back then, there was safety in numbers, and every member of a clan had something to contribute. Oral tradition was stronger, as it remains in some modern cultures. But that tradition is receding in many Western cultures, and this is what many senior members of the clan have to contribute to the clan. They can no longer hunt (or earn), nor can they procreate. All they have is the value of their experience, and it was right and proper that they share the lessons of that experience with younger generations. This practice was and remains central to US Native American Cultures, among others. So the senior members were valued and revered.

The modern Western cultures have largely replaced the oral tradition with other ways of recording their history; photo albums, home movies, for example. The only thing the senior member of the clan had to offer which was exclusive to them was this experience. True, grandparents can be sources of affection and love for grandchildren, but parents can provide affection. Home movies tell the stories of the past. And that leaves the grandchild and grandparent with little connection.

Most grandparents do delight in the presence of grandchildren, narcissistic personalities more than others. And this makes perfect sense. Infants and even young children offer everything the narcissist requires: unquestioned adoration, affirmation of an idealized self-image, an easy-to-manipulate intellect, physical control (despite a steadily decreasing physical strength). But as the grandchild ages, that relationship changes. The parent may lose control of their child, the grandparent is even more likely to do so.

Later in life, the grandchild and grandparent are all the more likely to become more distant as their lives travel in different directions and grandchildren go on to create their own lives and their own families. When the grandparent is a narcissist and in greater need, it's only natural that they would turn their narcissistic abuses on their grandchildren. Lacking the intimacy of the parent-child relationship, they can detach and become cruel. Their manipulative tactics can become abusive, particularly in the verbal and psychological realms.

It's too easy for a grandparent to compare the grandchild to their own adult child (the grandchild's parent). This parent may be deceased, leaving both grandparent and grandchild lacking and longing. This gives the aggrieved grandparent all the more license to be abusive, callous, even destructive to an already-damaged grandchild. When the grandparent is a narcissist, these abuses seem all the more natural and are almost certain.

The damage can be severe. Grandchildren are often trained to be obedient and respectful of their grandparents, and to be abused by them is a confusing and hurtful experience.

Transgenerational trauma is a little-known psychological concept which suggests that trauma can be handed down from one generation to the next.

Even post-traumatic stress disorder can be handed down in this way. And it can skip a generation. Grandparents can hand their traumas down to their grandchildren. This may be common when divorce has separated the child's parents. More than half of marriages in the United States in the Twenty-first century end in divorce. This can create a divide between the divorced parent's parents (paternal grandmother, let's say) and the child. If the mother divorced the father, the grandparent may project that onto the child, especially since most often the custody of children of divorce goes to the mother. Narcissists despise abandonment, and a paternal grandmother may well feel feelings of betrayal against her divorced daughter-in-law. As children are often raised by their divorced mothers, that sense of betrayal may transfer to the children. It's completely irrational, but remember that narcissists are expert at justifying their abuses, using them to reaffirm their idealized self-images.

Luckily, the adult grandchild can often simply cut the narcissistic elder out of their lives. If visiting them in the old folks home is unpleasant, just don't do it. True, we're trained to do at least perfunctory service for our elders. Elder abuse by neglect is a crime in the United States. Even failing to report it is a misdemeanor. Narcissistic seniors know this and can use it with expertise developed from a lifetime of manipulation. But nobody is honor-bound to be abused. Nobody has the right to be cruel, no matter how old they are.

The narcissistic senior will react harshly, using all their tricks to manipulate and control the grandchild. They may be given to histrionics, fits of self-pity, displaying behaviors of different complexes and abuses, perhaps sequentially. They won't be expecting frank disobedience. They may play the sobbing victim, the righteous martyr, the betrayed and vulnerable narcissist. As with other narcissistic relationships, the key to ending it is not to enable it. Narcissism is a trip meant for two, so just don't go there.

To do this, be prepared, have a plan, and stick to it. Draw the line and stand your ground, don't back down from it. Just walk away if that's what it takes.

Narcissistic grandparents may have another trick up their sleeves; financial abuse. Sure, we often think of seniors as reliant on their adult children, and they often are. But some collect considerable sums of money, and this may be the only instrument of control left to them. A juicy inheritance may be all the aged narcissist has to lord over their children or grandchildren. In this case, it's up to the victim to break the cycle if they dare. Which is more important, self-respect or old money? Hey, it could be a great deal of money in exchange for a few uncomfortable visits to a cranky old narcissist, so who's to say? But be prepared for this kind of manipulation.

How do you know if your grandparent is truly a narcissist and not just a cranky pain? Let's take a look at what makes a narcissist in the context of a grandparent.

We know narcissism presents as a sense of self-importance, often in a grandiose, exhibitionist fashion. The narcissistic grandparent will exhibit this trait with histrionic demonstrations of victimhood and martyrdom. As an elder in the bloodline, they may declare themselves necessary to the existence of subsequent generations, which to an extent may be true. It hardly means that their lives hinge on the elder, or that he or she is responsible for everything in the lives of subsequent generations, though they may desire to leave the other with this impression.

Narcissists have fantasies of their own unlimited brilliance, power, beauty, or ideal love. For the elderly, it's clear that they may lack several of these qualities, even to themselves. However, they may reach back to a time when they were powerful and beautiful and brilliant. And they can brilliance to experience, something they have more than others by virtue of their age. They may even turn their waning state on the grandchild. They may compete, pitting their younger, better selves against their grandchildren's present and even future selves.

Narcissists believe that they're special, and when contested they blame the natural inferiority of those who challenge them. Whether it's intergenerational differences or personal qualities of character, the narcissistic senior is apt to disqualify the opinions of the younger.

Narcissists need excessive admiration, and seniors do as well. They're often insecure, facing disease and death, and all they may have is the admiration of their families. And they deserve it. But when they demand it, in disproportionate supply, natural insecurity becomes narcissism.

This carries over to the narcissist's sense of entitlement. Age and survival alone may be just the tools the elderly narcissist needs, the one thing they have which others do not. And the elderly do deserve a certain amount of respect for the simple act of survival. Not everybody manages that, after all. Again, it's a matter of proportion and a matter of appeal. We all deserve things, but if somebody declares their entitlement they're likely to be a narcissist.

Narcissists are exploitative. If a grandchild is given to excessive exploitation of their grandchild, it's likely a manifestation of narcissism. They may do this by use of guilt and shame. They may be given to splitting, one of the most manipulative and exploitative acts in their canon. An exploitative elder may turn grandchildren against their parents or against their siblings.

Grandparents may have every good reason to demonstrate a lack of empathy. It's easy to play the victim, to be angry at everyone and everything, when you're as marginalized as many seniors are. But if they've become that bitter, that closed off to an emotional connection, it may be time to sever ties.

Narcissists are often charming, and a narcissistic grandparent may deliver such a performance. They're unlikely to be seductive, of course, but they can charm and manipulate by taking on different roles, as we've seen; victim, martyr. Madonna.

Narcissists are envious of others or they desire the envy of others. Modern-day seniors are unlikely to be the figures of others' envy. But it will be easy to find things to envy in others: Youth, financial control, personal freedom, good health. If a grandparent uses these things against a grandchild, you've got a narcissist.

Narcissist are arrogant, and this is a quality which seniors can readily adopt. It's the advantage of age and experience which can justify this, regardless of whether that age or experience has truly created greater wisdom, which is not always the case.

Seniors may be either grandiose or vulnerable narcissists, and in fact they may shift from one to another as their lives change. Getting older and weaker, losing the control they can no longer wield by grandiose measures, a senior may adapt vulnerable narcissism instead, retracting in order to seduce the attention they crave. In this case, it goes from admiration (grandiose) to pity (vulnerable) but it's still narcissism.

Narcissists overreact to criticism, and the elderly may exhibit this quality in spades. They're unlikely to receive criticism as a matter of general courtesy, but when they get it then they may go ballistic. It may be hard to say how much of this is narcissism and how much is reasonable upset, however.

A narcissistic grandparent will disrespect boundaries, as all narcissists do. They will ridicule life choices, holding them against their grandchildren. They will do the same to the middle generation, the parents/children, holding their dubious decisions against the grandchild. This grandparent may disrespect the boundaries of the parents and spoil the grandchildren at will, despite being told not to. They'll act entitled to do so when challenged and manipulate their kids into letting them do as they please. This is the way of the narcissist.

A narcissist is apt to think that they and only they are best qualified to make decisions, policies, protocols. And so, a narcissistic grandparent may try to intervene and raise the grandchild instead of the parent, asserting their seniority and superior abilities. Herein, they assault not the grandchild but the adult child-parent. But it's still narcissism, and it's still inappropriate. If this is your senior parent or parent-in-law, you'll have to assert your own authority as the child's parent.

The narcissist refuses to take responsibility, and this is something the narcissistic senior can do in many ways, Once again, feigning dementia or simple memory loss, it's easy to wipe away old events with impunity. If you're hoping for an apology from a narcissistic grandparent, don't hold your breath.

Narcissistic seniors, like all narcissists, need support, they need others who will adore and affirm their idealized self-image. These may be friends, relatives, even a favored child or grandchild. But if you're looking for a narcissist, look for the second.

Coping with a narcissistic grandparent has its own unique challenges. There's a natural type of respect which is customary between grandchildren and grandparents, but that's a one-way relationship. They may be disrespectful and expect respect in return. You can deny them, you can assert dominance, you can set limits. Unlike your connection to other narcissists, you have a certain flexibility. You as the grandchild could disengage if they fail to observe your boundaries. You can lord your new authority over them. Turn the tables. Why not? It's better than enabling them and continuing the cycle of their narcissistic abuse. Make your participation in their lives contingent upon respectful treatment. That's as much as anybody deserves, after all.

Make sure you have a support system of your own. If you're an adult grandchild dealing with a narcissistic grandparent, or an adult caught between a grandparent and grandchild, you likely have friends and associates of your own. Use them, rely on them, seek their guidance and advice. Being your own age in many cases, they're likely to have information you can use and they'll likely be happy to share it. Hey, that's what friends are for.

Always choose your battles wisely, and this is even more important when dealing with a narcissist and even more so with a narcissistic grandparent. But because they may fight at any instance. This is simply exhausting and it's pointless. You don't want to be bossed around or marginalized, but some things just aren't worth discussing. Roll your eyes, shake your head, and move on. And remember never to take it personally. The narcissist is never really talking about you, they're always talking basically like themselves.

But don't underestimate the senior narcissist. They wield the powers of the narcissist, after all, and can (and may) turn them against just about anyone. Be on your guard around any narcissist, even if it's your mother and the grandmother of your children, or your own grandmother.

My father's mother, my Grandmother Millie, lost her son and his family to a freak accident, and never fully recovered. Her grandchildren looked after her until her death. At least one of those grandchildren did prove to have NPD (and even sociopathy), he didn't exhibit those behaviors to any of his grandparents. And of the four grandparents we were raised with, only Millie exhibited any signs of real narcissism.

Or did she?

Remember that every case has to be taken on its own, that there are a number of external, often chaotic factors which can influence a person's behavior and any reasonable clinician's diagnosis.

After the death of her son, she wound up exhibiting troubling behaviors, including depression, memory loss, confusion, physical weakness. We finally had to put her into a series of controlled facilities, which she hated. Here is where her behavior became of value to us here and now.

She began to exhibit a lot of narcissistic behaviors. But were they narcissistic, or merely natural? She had a tendency toward histrionics, a martyr and a victim complex, but that seems fairly common in the very old, especially when they are not in control of their own living situation. Imagine yourself shunted away in such a place at the end of your life. You might feel victimized too. You might feel insecure, which is also what the narcissist feels.

But the two are not the same. Narcissist feel these things to an exaggerated, irrational degree. And while seniors in these conditions may be safer than they realize, their feelings of insecurity can be quite natural and forgivable.

She was given to grandiosity and self-importance, but it's easy to see that as a reaction to being marginalized, as seniors often are. It's easy to imagine that, as more millennials begin to care for their grandparents, this will become more common.

Old Millie often felt slighted and disrespected, and we were rarely disrespectful. She certainly felt mistreated, but then again, under the circumstances, it's hard not to sympathize and even empathize with anyone, cranky and nasty though she may be.

Narcissistic Grandchildren

Now, as ever, let's take a look at the flipside of the coin. As we've seen, childhood behaviors may be narcissistic in nature in a very basic sense. True narcissism comes with the intellectual maturity to deliberately indulge these behaviors, instead of instinctively.

But as children (and yes, even grandchildren) grow up, they must take responsibility for their behaviors (something a narcissist cannot do, as we've seen). And we've also noted the tendency of narcissism, NPD, and related disorders and complexes to be learned, handed down from one generation to the next and sometimes even skips a generation. So it's very likely that a situation may arise where a grandchild is the narcissist and the grandparent a victim. As narcissism is learned, and the most pervasive learning occurs from parent to child in the formative years. So it's possible that narcissism is learned by the parent, let's say the father, while the maternal grandparent may have no narcissistic tendencies at all.

This can be a treacherous situation. Here we have a senior, elderly, likely in many ways compromised (financially, socially, physically, mentally). Introduce to that a young, healthy narcissist, and it can lead to countless abuses. So let's turn our scrutiny to the elements of narcissism when applied to the case of the narcissistic grandchild.

In narcissistic grandchildren, the exaggerated self-importance may be expressed when the adult grandchild is responsible for the grandparent's security, legally or financially. Or they may lord their place as the future of the family, the grandparent's last, best chance at immortality. The or she may also position themselves as the gatekeeper of the senior's wellbeing in this way.

As a grandchild, the adult narcissist may revert to their childhood persona to play on their grandparent's sympathies and affections, the better to manipulate them. Manipulation is the key to the narcissist's power, after all.

The need for constant and excessive admiration and sense of entitlement can be cleverly used against the unwitting grandparent. A grandparent may have parental feelings of custody which linger from years before, and a manipulative young adult will know this and use it well.

The adult grandchild may have little reason to expect to be considered superior, or they may, depending on the approach. Remember that this relationship happens without the middle generation. That means the narcissistic grandchild can turn things against either absent parent from the middle generation. If this is the son or daughter of the victim grandparent, they can be manipulated in this way. If the narcissistic grandchild can assert that their parent was faulty, and if that parent was the progeny of the victim grandparent, it's like an extension of themselves. The parent's failure is like the grandparent's failure, in a way we've seen is all-too-easy to establish by the manipulative narcissist.

A narcissistic grandchild may exaggerate their own talents and achievements in the same way. Or they may go right for the throat and compare themselves and their positions in life with that of their victim grandparent. It's obviously not a fair comparison, but the narcissist excels at unfair comparisons. And a narcissist will assert their superiority at every turn.

The narcissistic fantasies of brilliance, power, perfect beauty, and brilliance, are also easy to adapt by an adult grandchild. Until this latest generation, as we've noticed, every generation has done better economically than the previous generation. So it was easy to compare one's self favorably against the previous generations. And as a senior's star wanes and a grandchild's star rises, these fantasies are even easier to assert and affirm.

The narcissistic grandchild, like most narcissists, has a superiority complex which gives them the propensity for snobbery and discounting others as inferior, due largely to the transactional nature of their worldview. So note behavior like judging the grandparent's friends, their memory, their lifestyle; anything which will marginalize them.

The narcissist is an exhibitionist, so the narcissistic grandchild may be grandiose in their behaviors. This should not be mistaken for outward attempts at volunteerism. I visited my grandmother at her convalescent hospital several times a week, lending my musical and artistic skills to their daily recreation time. My grandmother called me a showoff and chased me out virtually every single time.

A narcissistic grandchild may expect special favors, and inheritance is essentially the only thing a grandchild can manipulate a grandparent out of. This kind of manipulation includes aspects of financial and psychological abuse.

And all the while, the narcissistic grandchild may be ignoring the needs and feelings of the senior, writing them off as dementia or histrionics; functionally, a lack of empathy.

The narcissist keeps envy at the center of their worldview. But they narcissistic grandchild is unlikely to envy their grandparent. Instead, they will presume the envy of their grandparents. But if the grandparent is not a narcissist, as in this scenario, they're unlikely to have or to express envy for their own grandchild; pride, yes, envy, no.

A note about teenage grandchildren: We live in a world with diverse people in varying conditions. The so-called *nuclear family* is a rarity now, and different circumstances create differing families. It's not at all uncommon for a grandparent to raise a grandchild or to cohabitate with one. So the tricky teenage years should be addressed.

Much of what we said about adult grandchildren applies to teenage grandchildren. They're not likely to have any financial control over the senior, and they're all the more likely to inflict physical abuse. Otherwise, they may be prone to other abuses and manifestations of narcissism.

In the cases of either adult grandchild or teenage grandchild abuse of a grandparent, the common abuses may include substance abuse along with verbal, psychological, or identity abuses.

That covers what we'd consider the basic family unit. Narcissistic aunts, uncles, cousins and the like are all far enough removed to require such intense study. Use the same techniques that you would with a closer relative.

And speaking of techniques, that's just where our analysis leads us. But first, we turn our attention back to the spectrum of mental disorders, complexes, and conditions which are often concurrent with them. Then we'll know best how to treat the whole spectrum as they relate to family narcissism.

SECTION 3: OTHER, RELATED ABUSES AND DISORDERS

CHAPTER EIGHT: Other, Related Abuses and Disorders

Related Abuses

We've taken a look the differences between narcissism and narcissistic personality disorder. For this book's purposes, the abusive parent (and likely, to an extent, their children) may be either narcissistic or an NPD sufferer. We've seen how the symptoms can advance and progress, a disorder developing over time. We know these are basically learned conditions and disorders. Other, related conditions and complexes can develop along with NPD, interworking with it to create a web of mental ill-health. Looking closer at a narcissistic parent, you're likely to recognize some of these concurrent behavior sets. Recognizing them will help you deal with them effectively, even if you cannot correct them. While we've gone into this in great detail in our other book about narcissism and abuse, a good deal of the information is valuable here.

Narcissistic is designated a *Cluster B personality disorder,* which includes borderline personality disorder (BPD), antisocial personality disorder (APD), histrionic personality disorder (HPD), and attention-deficit/hyperactivity disorder (ADHD). Dissociative identity disorder (DID, previously known as multiple personality disorder), seems to fall into none of the clusters, but we'll discuss that in a moment in greater detail.

A personality disorder is a rigid and unhealthy way of functioning and thinking. They cause difficulty in relating to or understanding situations and people. The distorted perception may lead to limited personal relationships, social activities, as well as scholastic and workplace successes.

Other disorders, like NPD, often begin in childhood and develop through the teenage years. Symptoms may abate in middle age.

Personality disorders come in three clusters; A, B, and C. All feature insecurity, denial, and lack of empathy. Keep in mind that a patient needn't exhibit all of the behaviors in order to be clinically diagnosed.

Cluster A personality disorders feature very odd behaviors or thoughts, and includes includes schizoid personality disorder (SPD), paranoid personality disorder (PPD), and schizotypal personality disorder (STPD).

Symptoms of paranoid personality disorder include:

- Distrust in and suspicion of others and their true motives
- Belief that others are out to get them, to deceive them or otherwise damage them
- Doubt in the loyalty and trustworthiness of those close to them
- Closed to others, lacking intimacy, fearful that information will be used against them
- Holding grudges
- Suspect infidelity

The second Cluster A disorder is schizoid personality disorder. Contrary to popular assumption, this is not the condition known as multiple personality disorder. Rather than exhibiting different personalities, the schizoid presents a different set of behaviors:

- Disinterest in social or personal relationships
- Isolation
- Limited emotional expression
- Inability to enjoy moments or activities
- Inability to pick up normal social cues
- Indifference to others
- Little interest or disinterested in sexual intercourse

Schizotypal personality disorder shares some aspects of the others in the same cluster, and has some behaviors which are unique to it. Compare to the others and see if you recognize a pattern in recurring elements. The schizotypal personality disorder is identified by these behaviors:

- Strange thinking, behavior, dress, and speech
- Strange visual or audio hallucinations
- Flat or inappropriate emotions
- Social anxiety and discomfort with intimacy
- Indifference

- Suspicious or inappropriate responses
- Faith in mind control and subconscious messaging

The personality disorders in Cluster B are characterized by unpredictable, dramatic, or overly emotional thoughts and/or behaviors. Antisocial personality disorder (APD), histrionic personality disorder (HPD), borderline personality disorder (BPD), and narcissistic personality disorder (NPD).

Often called *sociopathology*, Antisocial personality disorder is known for a blatant disregard for other people's needs or feelings. It's known for:

- Use of aliases
- Persistent lying, conning, and stealing
- Recurrent legal problems
- Aggressive and/or violent behavior
- Irresponsibility
- Disregard for their own safety or the safety of others
- Impulsive
- Irresponsive
- Lacking remorse

Another Cluster B disorder is borderline personality disorder, another Cluster B disorder, one of the trickiest to diagnose and treat. Some therapists won't even try to treat it and turn away sufferers diagnosed with BPD. It's signaled by:

- Impulsive, risky behavior
- Unstable, intense relationships
- Fragile self-image
- Fear of abandonment
- Fear of being alone
- Extreme, drastic mood shifts, often stress-related
- Self-injury, suicide
- Feelings of emptiness
- Intense, frequent outbursts of rage
- Intermittent, stress-related paranoia

Histrionic personality disorder is notable for its sufferers' inclination toward seeking attention, among other histrionic and narcissistic traits:

- Attention seeking via excessive sexual or dramatic behaviors
- Given to diatribes and rants

- Lack the facts to support their diatribes and rants
- Rapidly shifting emotions
- Overestimation of closeness in personal relationships

Sadistic personality disorder (SPD) isn't listed in the DSM (nor is malignant narcissism, as you'll recall). There's little adolescent study of the disorder, singled by deriving joy from inflicting cruelty upon others and the witnessing the damage and suffering it causes. The disorder is commonly found concurrent with other disorders.

The other Cluster B personality disorder is narcissistic personality disorder, which presents with these behaviors:

- Delusions of power and superiority
- Expectation of praise and favoritism
- Envy
- Arrogance
- Lack of empathy
- A transactional mindset

Cluster C personality disorders are singled by fearful or anxious behavior or thinking. Avoidant, obsessive-compulsive, and dependent personality disorders are included in this cluster.

Avoidant personality disorder presents with these behaviors:

- Over-sensitivity to criticism or rejection
- Feelings of inadequacy, unattractiveness, and/or inferiority
- Work avoidance
- Social timidity
- Isolation
- Extreme shyness
- Fear of new people or situations
- Fear of disapproval, ridicule, or embarrassment

Dependent personality disorder is the next disorder in this cluster. It signals as:

- Excessive dependence
- Submissiveness
- Clinginess
- Fear of abandonment

- Requiring constant guidance and advice

- Lacking self-confidence

- Overthinking

- Inability to make choices

- Failure to start or complete projects

- Fear of disapproval

- Tolerance of abuse

- Excessive people-pleasing

- Fear of isolation

Among the most common and best-known is obsessive-compulsive personality disorder, signaled by:

- Obsession with orderliness, details and rules.

- Perfectionism and overthinking

- Control of situations, tasks, and other people

- Stubbornness and rigidity

- Moral and ethical inflexibility

- Spend-thriftiness

Note that that obsessive-compulsive personality disorder (OCPD) is distinct from obsessive-compulsive disorder (OCD), which is a type of anxiety (but not a personality) disorder. It's the belief in the rightness of their own behavior which makes it a personality disorder. Those who suffer but fight the condition are better diagnosed as having OCD.

Other Abusive Relationships

Narcissism is closely associated with abuses of various sorts, as we've already seen. So any comprehensive analysis must include at least a cursory look at these other abusive relationships, some of which are more closely related to narcissism than you may imagine. A narcissist may have any one (or several) of these other disorders and complexes, so the better you know them, the more equipped you'll be to handle them properly; and that's what this book is really about.

Sexual abuse, which includes rape and child molestation, presents as feeling of sexual inadequacy and sexual disfunction. Sexual situations offer trigger these feelings, though it's not always direct contact. A sexual abuser may be triggered merely by seeing an exotic dancer, the slightest social interaction with an attractive potential partner, even imagery on television, the internet, or perhaps a billboard. And once the feelings are triggered, they can be overwhelming and uncontrollable. The sexual abuser is often a narcissist, either grandiose or vulnerable. Substance abuse goes hand-in-hand with this type of abuse (as it does many others). And sexual abuse isn't limited to aggressive sexual behavior. Withholding sex, ridiculing a partner's sexual prowess or overestimating it to eclipse the person's other qualities of character are also aspects of sexual abuse.

Sexual abuse between parents and children, almost always with the child as the victim, includes incest, rape, child molestation. Of these, the last two are considered violent crimes in all 50 of the United States of America.

Physical abuse is another all-too-common type of abuse. Like a lot of the abuses here, it highlights violent transgressions like:

- Punching

- Kicking

- Physical restraint

- Spitting, biting, hair-pulling, etc.

But physical abuse may also include nonviolent transgressions such as:

- Drunk driving or reckless driving

- Exaggerated gesticulation

- Wild dancing

- Smoking cigarettes in pubic

The difference can be found in the motive. Violent abusers are generally motivated by anger, while non-violent abusers generally act out of a lack of empathy.

In the context of a parent-child relationship, physical abuse can take many forms. Unlike sexual abuse, physical abuse often occurs with the parent as the victim and the child as the perpetrator, as we've seen. This can take the form of punching, kicking, biting, throwing objects. Because of the age of the child, this is rarely considered criminal. However, it may escalate into attempted manslaughter or homicide in varying degrees. In some cases, murder in the first degree is often the charge, as in the case of California's infamous Menendez brothers.

Psychological abuse can be the most damaging in this cluster, as it is much more covert than sexual or physical abuse. The victim may not even realize they've been abused and so may never seek treatment. The abuser may also not be aware that such a thing as psychological abuse even exists and are also unlikely to abate or control the behavior. Psychological abuse often goes hand-in-hand with physical and sexual abuse and substance abuse as well. Passive/aggressive behavior is also common to this kind of abuse. Psychological abuse can contain any number of abuse behaviors, such as gaslighting; this is the process of deliberately confusing someone until they doubt their own perceptions of reality.

Psychological abuse in a parent-child relationship often manifests as:

- Guilt
- Shame
- Unfair treatment
- Belittling

- Marginalization
- Gaslighting

Verbal abuse is also a kind of strain of psychological abuse. It's common among authoritative types as narcissistic device to maintain control over others. Verbal abuse is also a staple of identity and even financial abuse. It can go along with sexual and physical abuse as well. Verbal abuse is common in child-parent relationships, and it may include the same signals as psychological abuse.

Economic and financial abuse is common to narcissists, and very common in child and parent abuse. Money is controlled as a way of controlling the victim. Spouses inflict this type of abuse on one another as well.

In a child-parent relationship, financial abuse is especially prevalent. It may include denial and theft of resources, as we've discussed.

Cultural (or identity) abuse is the marginalization of anything cultural or racial. These things may include:

- Racial slurs

- Gender discrimination by incrimination or denial
- Ridiculing religions or languages
- Foods
- Films/entertainment
- Hygiene
- Clothing
- Stereotypes of any kind

Cultural slurs are not as common in child-parent relationships, and that's for an obvious reason. Members of the same family generally share cultural practices and institutions. This isn't always the case, however. Teenagers and adult children often adopt different cultural practices from those they were raised with. Religious conversions, shifts in philosophy, insight to the human condition; all are common in the teenage years and beyond. It can happen to parents too, who may respond to the infamous *midlife crisis* with drastic shifts in lifestyle.

But identity abuse is still common in families. It happens when a parent compares on child to another, marginalizes their personality or qualities of character, or engage in other verbal and psychological abuses. Gaslighting may also be considered a form of identity abuse.

People often react to gaslighting by evincing the following traits or behaviors.

- Increased anxiety
- Over-sensitivity
- Insecurity
- Emptiness
- Doubt

Attention-deficit/hyperactivity disorder (ADHD) presents as a pattern of hyperactivity and impulsivity and/or inattention which creates maldevelopment or social dysfunction. It's often found in children, who because of various factors are diagnosed with the disorder. Sadly, sugary cereals and drinks set most kids off in a falsely energetic mood, and this combines with their natural, youthful energy. Add to this a lack of regulated exercise, too much sedentary time in front of the TV or computer, and any number of normal and even healthy childhood behaviors may be misdiagnosed as

ADHD. Chronic or uncontrolled behavior is a red flag of any disorder.

Actual ADHD can be signaled by:

- Lacking persistence
- Inability to complete tasks
- Extreme disorganization
- Lack of comprehension
- Constant, uncontrollable movement not caused by neurological dysfunction
- Uncontrolled speaking
- Self-harm
- Overlooking details
- Inattentiveness
- Failure to organize
- Avoidance
- Easily distracted
- Unexpected exits
- Unnecessary running or dashing
- Loudness
- Interrupting
- Impatience

Risk factors for ADHD may include:

- Genetics

- Exposure to substance use (cigarette smoke, alcohol, drugs) during pregnancy

- Exposure to external (environmental) poisons or toxins during pregnancy

- Brain injury

- Low birth weight

ADHD is less commonly reported in females than in males.

Like other disorders, there's no real cure, but psychoanalysis and medication are ways to manage the disease and control the symptoms and related behaviors. Family therapy is often a remedy of choice for clinicians and psychoanalysts. Maintaining an organized schedule is a good way to curb ADHD in children, as they crave and require organization and control, things they cannot provide on their own.

Under medical supervision, stimulant medications are considered safe. However, there are risks and side effects, especially when misused or taken in excess of the prescribed dose. For example,

stimulants can raise blood pressure and heart rate and increase anxiety. Therefore, a person with other health problems, including high blood pressure, seizures, heart disease, glaucoma, liver or kidney disease, or an anxiety disorder should tell their doctor before taking a stimulant.

If you're prescribed medication for ADHD or any disorder, be aware of the common side effects, including:

- Sleep problems
- Decreased appetite
- Twitches and ticks
- Irritability and anxiety
- Mood shifts
- Personality changes
- Headaches
- Stomach aches

Now let's take a minute to look at the mysterious and confusing dissociative identity disorder (DID). Formerly known as *multiple personality disorder*, DID is a complex mental condition which is often the result of abuses in childhood. It presents as discontinuous thoughts, feelings, actions, and sense of identity. Childhood trauma occurring before age six is reported to play a part in almost all cases of DID. It presents with these symptoms:

- At least two and likely more distinct personality states (often as many as 15)
- Inability to recall key personal information
- Distinct and fluctuating memories
- Hallucinations
- De-realization (misperception of reality)
- Perceived out-of-body experiences (detachment)
- Amnesia
- Headaches
- Self-sabotage
- Self-persecution
- Various personality complexes
- Violence, both outwardly directed and inwardly directed
- Disavowing responsibility

Like a lot of disorders (though whether this is a personality disorder remains arguable), DID features concurrent conditions, including:

- Depression
- Suicidal tendencies
- Substance abuse
- Eating disorders

There's some question as to what cluster Post-traumatic stress disorder falls under, but it certainly requires some study here. Certainly, parental abuse creates PTSD, which can manifest in a number of ways, all of them harmful and some debilitating.

Unlike most disorders, which originate in childhood, PTSD may originate from adult trauma as well as childhood trauma. Various abuses at any time in life may cause PTSD. It's also known to originate from non-abuse events such as random violence (criminal but not abusive) or natural disaster, war events, or other sudden traumas. During World War I, the condition was known as being *shell-shocked*. PTSD may present in the following ways:

- Close proximity to inciting incident

- Amnesia of the event

- Flashbacks of the event

- Substance abuse

- Isolation

- Depression

- Stunted growth in social, professional, and intimate relationships

- Mood swings

- Temper tantrums and angry outbursts

Related complexes

Now that we've looked at other disorders and how they relate to child-parental abuses, let's take a look at related complexes. These are important to understand they many may be present in the narcissistic abusive parent or adult child. Recognizing these complexes will go a long way toward helping you know what you're dealing with and how to deal with it. Luckily, unlike disorders, complexes can be reversed. But like the disorders, the sufferers often don't know or won't acknowledge their dysfunctionality.

Like disorders, psychological complexes are distorted thought patterns which lead to behaviors which are considered aberrant or unnatural. Also like disorders, complexes are deep-rooted in childhood, not genetics, and are developed through time. Though, like disorders, they may be accompanied by certain genetic traits, like temperament and personality type. Also, like disorders, complexes are likely to get worse with time.

In the Oedipus/Electra complex, the sufferer has a romantic inclination toward the opposite-gender parent (Oedipus with a son and his mother, Electra with a daughter and her father). Both are likely to result in a series of unsuccessful, unhappy relationships marked by dissatisfaction generated by unrealistic, unhealthy expectations.

In the context of the child-parent relationship, this complex is one of the most common and most directly applicable. Parents with the complex, particularly in an Electra-type relationship, may abuse the adoration they're nurturing and encourage a sexual connection. It's terribly abusive and the epitome of narcissism, in parenting and in social interaction in general. The narcissistic parent gets everything they need from the relationship, including unquestioned adoration, fawning affection, undying loyalty, complete control, a relationship where empathy is not needed because obedience is absolute. If this type of relationship continues, it can become criminal all too quickly.

In the Oedipal version, the mother may manipulate the son's love and loyalty and challenge his romantic prospects to maintain control and ensure codependency.

The God complex presents as the sufferer's feelings that they are above reproach, that they possess godlike powers. It's an extreme form of the superiority and hero complexes, as well as grandiose narcissism, NPD, and histrionic personality disorder. Characteristics of this complex include perfectionism, blaming, shaming, a generally demanding nature.

In a child-parent situation, the God complex is most likely to strike the parent, but this is not always the father. The father may insinuate themselves as the unquestionable head of the household, a god in that realm for all intents and purposes. It's a while you're under my roof kind of approach, all too common in households all over the world. Mothers may utilize the guilt and they martyr complexes in conjunction with the God complex. It was the mother who carried the child, as we've discussed, who gave life, as a god might do.

The Madonna/whore most often strikes heterosexual men who see women as being one of two idealized images of womanhood; that of the sinful, lustful whore and those of the virtuous virgin Madonna. They sometimes desire a combination of both in one, alternating between a whore in the bedroom and a Madonna in the nursery. The problem is that sufferers of this complex can often not digest the dichotomy, if they manage to get it, which is unlikely. They resent the whore for her lofty Madonna airs, and they are made to feel guilty for defiling their Madonna when in the bedroom.

But, of course, no woman is both Madonna and whore any more than any man is God. This one isn't very common to parent-child relationships, though it can overlap with the Oedipus complex, wherein the son idealizes the mother as a Madonna figure. This may come into play when the mother is single (or widowed or divorced) and it's the son who is the narcissist. They may resent their Madonna-like mothers for pursuing whore-like relationships with other men who is not their father. They may be so resistant to the notion of anyone violating that Madonna image that they're personally threatened, regardless of feelings for the absent father. Also, when the child is the narcissist, and we've seen this begins at a young age, their need for singular devotion and fear of abandonment may be even more deep-rooted. Because these are irrational fears, and children are naturally more emotional and less rational, the narcissistic behaviors may be all the more egregious in these cases.

The persecution complex gives sufferers an irrational fear of being persecuted or otherwise poorly treated. It's often seen in conjunction with paranoid personality disorder and the martyr complex. It appeals to vulnerable narcissists as well, and presents with feelings of persecution, mistrustfulness, and isolation.

In the context of a parent-child relationship, the persecution complex may be adopted by either the parent or the child. A child may feel persecuted early in life, and an abused parent may feel the same way later in life. In point of fact, if either is dealing with a narcissist, they may not be wrong. But that treatment can certainly encourage the development of persecution complex, a martyr complex, or a guilt complex.

The superiority complex finds sufferers considering themselves basically superior to others, as in the God and hero complexes, NPD, and both grandiose and vulnerable narcissism. It's association with vulnerable narcissism may surprise you, but remember that the vulnerable narcissist still believes themselves superior, even when it's not adoration they feel their entitled to, but harsh treatment and rejection.

A superiority complex, like many of the disorders and behavioral maladies we're looking at in this and our other books, is developed throughout early life and tends to get worse. A superiority complex in a child can easily develop into narcissism later, then into full-fledged narcissistic personality disorder. Add a growing comfort with sadism and you've got a sociopath on your hands.

The inferiority complex is (predictably) the opposite of the superiority complex. Sufferers consider themselves inadequate and unable to meet life's challenges. They're very often vulnerable narcissists but sometimes grandiose narcissists as well. Remember that all types of narcissism are rooted in tremendous insecurity on the part of the narcissist. suffered by those who consider themselves gravely inadequate to meet the challenges of life. Avoidant and paranoid personality disorders are often found alongside the inferiority complex.

This complex rears its head in child-parent relationships whenever narcissism is involved. This is because the narcissist has to be superior (even the vulnerable narcissist feels this in their way). So if the narcissistic parent is superior (and transactional in this superiority) the child must therefor be inferior. When instilled early on through various verbal, psychological, and various other abuses, the inferiority complex can be devastating and long-lasting. The guilt complex is rarely found far from the inferiority complex.

The martyr complex is notable for attracting sympathy and attention through the outward expression of suffering. This dovetails with histrionic personality disorder for its drama, grandiose for its exhibitionism, paranoid personality disorder for its sense of unending persecution.

The martyr complex, when found in parent-child relationships, is most common found in the parents, particularly the mother. It's an inherently narcissistic complex and relates to histrionic and paranoid personality disorders. It tends to generate guilt complexes in children.

The guilt complex belongs right next to the martyr complex. They're largely similar, but sufferers of this complex tend to blame themselves for their suffering, whereas the martyr needs a person to sacrifice themselves for and others to blame for it. In other words, the martyr is innocent; the guilty is, well guilty. It's commonly found alongside grandiose narcissism and histrionic personality disorder, and perfectionism.

Since guilt is rarely experienced by narcissists, this complex arises from parent-child relationships often manifests in the abused party, not the abuser. It is often associated with depression, isolation, substance abuse, poor sleep patterns and dietary habits, ill-health, premature death, and suicide.

Those disorders are also usually found in close proximity to the hero complex. Like those with the martyr complex, sufferers of the hero complex need somebody to fight for and somebody else to fight against. Firefighters, paramedics, police officers, politicians, and even psychologists may fall into the complex due to occupational hazards. The hero complex is closely related to grandiose narcissism and NPD.

The hero complex is likely to manifest in parents, alongside complexes like martyr, superiority, and God. The head of the household is likely to consider themselves the hero of the family, and to lord that over the children. That's particularly irrational, as no child can be expected to run a household. Simply attending to one's legal responsibilities hardly makes anyone a god, but it remains a good way to manipulate a child's mind, especially in the home where they are trained not to question their elders.

The Don Juan complex presents as womanizing, fleeting relationships, disrespect of women as little more than objects of the gratification and pleasure of men. It may be related to grandiose narcissism, but of the overt type. Those with the Don Juan complex do like to draw attention to themselves, and the very nature of the complex echoes elements of superiority, hero, and God complexes as well.

The Don Juan isn't closely associated with the parent-child relationship or other, related abuses. Certain rare exceptions may apply. But outside of a soap opera, the Don Juan complex manifests itself as behaviors associated with other disorders. It has the exhibitionism of grandiose narcissism, the relationship superficiality of sexual abuse and various personality disorders.

Infamous Cases

While we're here to talk about child-parental abuses, looking at these other types of abuses and disorders was and remains crucial to our understanding of the full spectrum of related disorders. And how better to understand them than some well-known public examples. It helps to illustrate the depth of the problem and the related behaviors.

Actors Johnny Depp, Sean Penn, Mel Gibson, actress Stacey Dash, and others have reportedly faced abuse-related charges. Bill Cosby is currently serving prison time for his convictions of sexual abuse. Singer Rick James did too. Actress Emma Roberts faced arrest on charges of domestic violence against Even Peters. Singer Chris Brown faced charges of beating singer Rihanna. Nicolas Cage faced arrest for disturbing the peace and domestic battery.

But it's not just about domestic abuse. Mental health issues of a variety of sorts are found across the spectrum of world fame and notoriety.

According to the best online records, it seems that model and television personality Chrissy Teigen suffered from post-partum depression (as did former supermodel and actress Brooke Shields); Demi Lovato came forward to online sources with stories of addiction, bullying, cutting, depression, and an eating disorder. NFL Hall of Famer Steve Young is reported as having social anxiety disorder, as has former teen idol Donny Osmond. American swimmer Michael Phelps is reported as having attention-deficit-hyperactivity-disorder (ADHD). Actors Leonardo di Caprio and Daniel Radcliff are reported as having obsessive-compulsive disorder. According to a 2014 interview, pop singer and actress Lady Gaga suffered from post-traumatic stress disorder from a rape committed against her in her late teens.

Whew! This brings us to the darkest depths of our journey so far. We've gone down that proverbial rabbit hole with the narcissist, the abuser, the victim. From this point, we're heading toward the light at the end of this deep, dark tunnel.

Now we're ready to talk about remedies. True, we talked about dealing with certain types of people and even different remedial moves in general, it's time to get clinical. Some of what we've looked at cannot be cured (BDL) only managed, others (narcissism) can be treated and even cured. Knowing the difference will make all the difference in the effectiveness of your ultimate course of action, whatever it may be. So read on, knowing that every page, every paragraph, brings you or your loved one closer to healing, to happiness.

SECTION 4: RECOVERIES

CHAPTER NINE: Recovering from Emotionally Abusive Relationships

Recoveries; there are plenty of them, different ones for different reasons. They get quite clinical, but they're important to understand and we've taken steps to make that understanding easy and effective. But those are specific applications, and to understand them let's take a quick look at something a bit more general.

Emotional abuse is a sort of an umbrella term used to cover relationships marked by abuses. If you've had a relationship with a narcissist or someone with NPD, you're virtually certain to have had an emotionally abusive relationship. Other disorders are likewise inherently abusive, their sufferers are prone to inflicting abuse. It's how they wield their power. All abuses have emotional impact. This is so because the rational mind can resist abuses with intellectual responses, but the emotional self can only react.

But not all abuses are the same, not all reactions are the same, and not all approaches are best. However, there is enough consistency to address them all, for our purposes, as emotionally abusive relationships. They can be addressed with some consistency as well.

As we've seen, emotionally abusive relationships have certain hallmarks.

Lack of empathy is recurrent in emotionally abusive relationships of virtually every sort. This is so because if an abuser had any empathy, they wouldn't likely be an abuser. But this can shift when looking at the sufferer of the guilt or victim complexes, who may actually seek abuse themselves. But really, they're manipulating others into those roles so they can fulfill their own, so who's really the victim and who is the abuser?

Marginalization is common to all abusive relationships, as is the idealized self-image of the abuser. These are the core concepts which allow and justify the abuses. A combination of insecurity and superiority is common as well. Common emotionally abusive tactics include verbal abuses like constant criticism, insults and shaming, gaslighting and other mind games, retraction, and isolation/splitting.

Emotionally abusive relationships are notable also for the recurrent cycle of abuse, of whatever sort: It begins with calm or friendliness, progresses to tension/anger which results in the explosion of uncontrolled abuse. Contrition ends the cycle so that it may start again on a calm or friendly note. Each of these stages, you'll note, is meant to keep the victim off their footing, to confuse them with a fluid state of things, uncertain as to what's happening or what's going to happen next.

Anxiety, depression, stress, and PTSD are common side-effects of emotionally abusive relationships.

So whatever the particulars of any emotionally abusive relationship, let's turn our attention from identification to recovery.

As we've discussed, remove yourself from the equation. It's not about you, so accept no blame in your own heart and mind. Now let's get a bit more particular.

Before that's said, the fact is that in some cases, there can be no cure, only recovery from a defunct relationship. There may be management with no real recovery (anti-social disorder). The best way to recover from a degenerative mental condition is to prevent it. The best way to escape an abusive relationship is to never get into it.

But this isn't always so easy. Abusive relationships are degenerative with time, and the change may be insidious. Narcissists are charmers. Abusers integrate their abuses gradually. To prevent such things from developing requires preparation, education, and sadly these are things we usually only seek once prevention is too late. So preventing abusive relationships requires tools and time that most people just don't have at their disposal.

Often, recovery is the only way.

First of all, don't rush your recovery from an emotionally abusive relationship. These relationships are likely to be long-standing, after all. If they're familial relationships, which is the focus of this book, then these relationships have probably lasted your whole life (less in the case of stepparents). Hardly matters, that's still going to be a long time with a person meant to be an intimate. So the recovery will not be swift nor will it be easy.

Emotionally abusive relationships are often treated with psychoanalysis of whatever school (narrative therapy, cognitive-behavioral, dynamic-behavioral) and these are often extended campaigns which can take months or even years. Emotionally abusive relationships are complex, with different complexes and disorders at play. Sorting them all out will take time even before real recovery begins. These problems weren't created overnight and they won't be solved overnight.

Sorry.

Be ready to redraw your boundaries. True, the narcissist in particular and the abusive person in general will care nothing for your boundaries and will trample all over them (while zealously guarding their own), this isn't for the narcissist, it's for you. Remember, we're not talking about dealing with the narcissist; this chapter is about recovering from the relationship. So let's assume you've gotten out and now you're rebuilding. Boundaries will be key to preventing another abusive relationship from being created. Did you just get out of an emotionally abusive relationship with a substance abuser? Your new boundaries may exclude substance use from your life. A financially abusive relationship may inspire you to redraw your personal boundaries to exclude anybody's access to your personal resources.

And this only makes sense. They say the definition of insanity is doing the same thing the same way and expecting a different outcome. Anybody would want to learn from their mistakes.

This can sometimes be unfair to the next relationship. If you've had an emotionally abusive relationship with an actor, let's say (very often narcissists) you might redraw your boundaries to exclude actors. But not all actors are narcissists, and you (or anyone) might be closing their minds and hearts to new and unexpected possibilities. Note that this is the development of the fixed mindset (all actors are narcissists) which inhibits growth and experience through change and risk.

Be the advocate of your own selfcare. Lord knows the narcissist won't help you do it! You have to look out for yourself, and that means investigating the different therapies to find out which will be most effective for you. You'll want to research therapists for specialties, experience, personal manner and style. You'll need to work hard and educate yourself. And most of all you'll have to accept the fact that you do need help (if you do). There's no shame, in fact it's a matter of self-awareness, self-regulation, and (ultimately) self-actualization, all things an emotionally abusive relationship will seek to curb.

Accept the fact that you will never have a relationship with this person again. Let go of hope, as it can plague you. As we've said, once you take your position and stand your ground, you have to hold it. In this case, since you're already gone, it's important to stay away. They may be reaching out with contrition, eager to start the cycle again. The may promise you that they've learned their lesson, that they've changed. They may simply rely on the passage of time to have cured the problem. Resist this. But be fair. Even the worst disorders can be managed. If your narcissist has undergone the necessary clinical, perhaps even inpatient therapies, you may reconsider. But do it with caution and not without significant, verifiable work on the narcissist (or other abuser's) behalf.

Abusers of any stripe are control-centered. It is both their motivation and their goal. So in their absence, you will have to assume control or somebody else is likely to come along and do it. If you've learned anything from a recent emotionally abusive relationship (hopefully you learned more than that, thanks to this book), it's that a sense of control is necessary to any stable psyche and any happy, satisfied life. Self-regulation, self-awareness, active listening, clear communication, rational responses instead of emotional reaction; all of these are about control.

And if you've been in an emotionally abusive relationship, you may have fallen into patterns which may make you reliant on others. Financial control is an easy way for one person to control another, and it can be a difficult thing to take control of. Finances can become complex; taxes, payrolls, inheritences. If you're coming out of a financially abusive relationship, you may not have any more finances to speak of. Or your finances could be in such a mess that you feel overwhelmed.

Take control.

Emotions overwhelm us too, especially after such abusive relationships. We don't know if we can trust our own emotions in this case. We've seen that this is a common (and intended) result of abusive behavior. Remember that the human psyche cannot be both emotional and rational at the same time. Use reason to counter emotion. You may want to employ certain relaxation techniques such as meditation, to help self-regulate your emotions.

Different therapies can be effective, and we'll take a closer look at those in a moment. But in general, you may try individual, couples, or group therapy. Workshop formats and retreats can be effective too.

When we do talk about therapies, we'll touch on narrative therapy. In short, this is a matter of reframing things to recast the role of the client in events. A victim in an abusive relationship may see themselves as a perpetual victim, playing their part in a natural cycle. They may have a fixed mindset which tells them that they will always have to play this role.

Don't get locked into this fixed mindset. Adapt a growth mindset and believe that nobody is assigned to any roles, nor to any fate. Changes are possible. The first step of change is, frankly, to change. Change creates is own cycle. Change your way of speaking and you will change your way of thinking. Change your way of thinking and you will change your behavior. Chane your behavior and you change the other two. It doesn't really matter where in the cycle you begin, just get in and break it.

Change is the only constant, and it's probably your first, best chance of recovery from an emotionally abusive relationship.

Don't fall back in with another abuser. You may swear that you've learned, that you've changed. And you probably have. But that doesn't mean the same elements in your personality which allowed the first abusive relationship aren't still there. As you work toward changing them, be aware of abusive behaviors and realize you have to stay away from them. Once again, self-awareness and self-regulation.

The Four Stages of Healing from Abuse

So while you're being patient and going through the necessary steps to recover from an emotionally abusive relationship, what can you expect? How can you chart your progress? Be aware of these four stages of recovery and you'll know what to expect. If you're not making the progress you'd hoped, maybe you're stuck in one of these stages. Knowing them will help you get through them and move onward toward your full and complete recovery.

Stage one is to acknowledge the abuse. Acknowledge to yourself that you've been a victim, and this may not be easy. Aside from a few sufferers from complexes we've looked at, nobody wants to think of themselves as a victim. Sure, it may make failures easy to handle, but we'd all generally prefer to have successes. In the United States in particular, there is a cultural can-do attitude which is closely associated to the ethos of achievement. In the United States, the victim may be seen as a loser, and that kind of identity association leads to abuses of the sort, fixed-mindedness, and other forms of self-sabotage.

Even so, people can be victimized without being victims. Remember to externalize the person from the circumstance or even the behavior. Over the curse of a lifetime, a person is likely to win and to lose, to be accepted by some and rejected by others. This does not make a person a lifetime winner or loser. A growth mindset, you'll recall, holds failure as a part of the process of success. A win doesn't necessarily make a winner, a loss doesn't necessarily make anybody a loser.

Being victimized doesn't make a person a victim. It happens. And it's no reflection on the victim. Abusers are expert at their abuses, spending lifetimes perfecting their strategies and manipulations. More often than not, a victim has not spent years becoming a victim. They're likely to be unprepared for what's happening, even unaware of it. This stems from innocence, not ignorance. So there's no shame in it, though it may be easy to look back in hindsight and have self-directed anger or regret. Get through this first stage of self-forgiveness will put you well on your way to recovery.

Stage two is determination to recover. Once you have admitted that there was a problem, you have to commit to a remedy. Keep that new growth-mindset and don't let anything stop you. Your recovery may include new lifestyle choices, therapies, other proactive steps, It may require painful reflection and reliving early pains, considering contemporary views. You may be tempted to back away from your campaign, to declare yourself cured somewhere in this stage. This is when you may be most tempted to convince yourself you've skipped ahead. Don't. You can't skip over the steps here, they're sequential, and they only get more challenging.

Note that recovering sufferers from emotionally abusive relationships may fall quicky into another relationship, even one which is not abusive. While it may be better to spend most of one's recovery time alone, this can take months or years and that can be a long time to turn possible relationships away. New relationships and partners can help with the recovery process. But be open and honest with them about your previous abusive relationship and your current recovery. Seek to make them a part of your recovery, and use clear communication and empathy, make a mutual plan and stick to it. Note that a new relationship will be vulnerable during the recovery process of a previous relationship. It may not survive, and that's a shame. But that's why it may be better to pursue recovery alone, or with a non-romantic recovery partner such as a good friend or professional therapist, support group, or other support system.

Stage three is marked by the powerful compassion you will feel as your recovery progresses. Working through the sources of your own pain will manifest as a new understanding for the suffering of others. This escalated empathy is a real mark of progress. And this is so even if you considered yourself fairly empathetic to begin with. At this point, you may begin to have new empathy for the former, abusive partner. This will come with greater understanding of their own pain, the reasons for their abusive behavior. That's not to say you'd be willing to return to the relationship. On the contrary, you're moving onward, away from that relationship. But as you give them your empathy, you can let go of the anger and guilt and shame. After all, somebody with a personality disorder or extreme abuses aren't entirely to blame for their actions. They suffer from terrible diseases of the mind. They're not to be excused, but to forgive them will be a positive step toward self-actualization and complete recovery.

Stage four is highlighted by being a model to others. Very often, in cases of recovery, the client will go on to help others. This is common in the twelve-step Alcoholics Anonymous program, where recovering alcoholics will sponsor new members. This is both part of their maintenance regiment and part of the program's methodology for propagating itself. Those who have worked the program are especially suited to help others through it. They know the challenges, the pitfalls. They have the experience to help others achieve success. And it's basically the same thing with other types of recovery. They say we best lead by example, and we're best positioned to set an example after recovery. Others may need the help, after all. And without the leadership of the experienced, less available help means fewer recoveries and a less-healthy community and society.

The recovered abuse victim may have other, more selfish reasons to help others. When the problem persists in one's social circle, it remains a looming threat. Relapse is always a possibility. Maintaining one's focus on healthy relationships is a good way to prevent relapse, but removing the triggers and influences will go a long way too. A recovering alcoholic is particularly vulnerable to relapsing under the influence of close friends, who set the example contrary to the one the recovering abuse victim is. Justifications, excuses, all manner of self-sabotage may come into play, until the recovery is undone and the abuse cycle is re-established.

You'll also win the respect of others who can see that, not only were you determined to help yourself, you're just as committed to helping others. And they don't have to be your friends (probably best if they're not, lest you seem like you're trying to change them against their wills). Volunteer with a variety of support groups, easy to find online in just about every city in the United States and other countries all over the world.

Recovering from Co-dependency

As we've seen, co-dependency is a big part of a lot of the abusive relationships we've looked at. And it figures into the various therapies too. But it's also a kind of umbrella term, to refer to a condition within an abusive relationship. Not all abusive relationships are co-dependent, but it happens often enough and in a devastating variety of ways. So let's get straight to some of the best ways to deal with co-dependency. You'll probably find that these techniques integrate to the others we'll look at in greater detail in the next chapter.

First, if you're in a co-dependent relationship with an abuser, remind yourself that the relationship is not central to your happiness. A co-dependent partner may be able to rationalize staying in the relationship by feeling they just can't live without it.

Either for fear of being alone, knowledge of being imperfect, or due to the manipulations of the abuser which make the victim feel unworthy, the co-pendent party may feel that they'll never do better. But this person must come to the realization that, not only can they be happier in another relationship, that's the only way they're going to be happier. And that happiness is compatible with an abusive partner, co-dependence or not.

The abused party must learn to externalize intimacy from romance. It sounds counterintuitive. But there are other kinds of intimacies. The co-dependent victim needs to replace the abusive relationship with one which has as much intimacy as the abusive relationship. But this intimacy can be found in good friends, family members. It comes from trust, sharing, shows of physical affection (not necessarily romantic affection). The problem here is that the co-dependent partner may have lost sight of the difference, and the abusive partner would know this and use it. Convincing the abused partner that romantic intimacy is the only kind of intimacy puts the abuser in a perfect position to control the flow of intimacy into the abused party's life. If it's a monogamous romance, a psychologically abusive person will use this to starve the partner of the affection they might need. This, as we've seen, is a form of sexual abuse as well (denial of intimacy).

The flipside of this that co-dependent abuse victims are often being controlled by their abusive partners, and this means rarely having time alone. Time alone cannot be controlled or governed, which makes it a threat. So to get free of co-dependence, the aggrieved party should spend more time alone. Reconnection to personal ideals, meditation, reflection, consideration, digesting information, making plans, strategizing and effectuating those plans; these are often solitary endeavors. They certainly require self-awareness, self-regulation, and self-confidence. These are best perfected alone, and over long periods. It's not to say a co-dependent person has to become a hermit, just the opposite. But an effort should be made to re-integrate private time to allow for regular reflection and a renewed connection to one's self.

And when you're reconnecting with yourself, be forgiving. Do not spend this time blaming yourself, overthinking the relationship's failure, falling into a fixed mindset which may convince anyone that they have no chance at happiness (which was probably just what the abuser wanted). Use this time to explore new experiences or pursuits, to reconnect with the best of your behaviors and thoughts; focus on the present, not the past and not the future.

As we said, looking for intimacy is a good way to get over co-dependence as long as you're not simply replacing one abusive relationship for another. But while you're looking for more romantic intimacy, be mindful of the platonic intimacy in your life. When you find romantic intimacy again, resist the temptation to ignore your other relationships. It's natural to become enthralled to a new lover, but your friends and family cannot be shunted. This is just a narcissistic splitter will want. You may even be encouraging such a thing, but that's just another big step down the road to co-dependency and abuse.

And you'll regret it if you lose your friends' intimacy the next time you need it, and you probably will.

We're getting closer to our goal now, a safe and reliable way to put any victim of narcissism or abuse back on secure footing. Now that we know what are the popular therapies and their generally most effective applications, let's tighten our focus upon emotionally abusive relationships the like of which we've been looking at here.

CHAPTER TEN: The Best Therapies for Recovery from Emotionally Abusive Relationships

Psychotherapy, often called the talking cure, is a popular and effective way to treat all manner of mental conditions and challenges. It's especially good for recovery of emotionally abusive relationships (as opposed to psychopharmaceutical, for instance). Psychotherapy focuses on coming to an understanding about previous causes of current conditions. It can be cathartic, enlightening, and difficult. And there are different schools of psychotherapy, each with a different emphasis.

Cognitive-behavioral therapy (CBT) is one of the most widely practiced types of psychotherapy. It focuses on connections between the client's (or patient's) behavior and their thoughts and feelings. It explores thoughts and feelings as causal to behavior. Cognitive-behavioral therapy holds that if the thoughts and thought patterns can be changed, the behavior can then be more easily modified, no matter how self-destructive those behaviors may be. In fact CBT is often used to deal with substance abuse problems, self-harm, and other destructive behavior patterns. CBT is a common treatment for depression, anxiety disorders, eating disorders, bipolar disorders, schizophrenia, and trauma-related behaviors.

Dialectical behavior therapy (DBT) shares a lot with CBT. Dialectical focuses on emotional patterns than thought patterns, accepting some thought patterns rather than trying to change them. Cognitive may focus more on change, and dialectical focuses more on acceptance. It's often used for hard-to-treat conditions like borderline personality disorder and suicidal personality disorder. DBT is also proven effective for treatment of post-traumatic stress disorder, eating and substance abuse disorders, and mood disorders.

Interpersonal therapy focuses on interrelationships with others, making it ideal for those recovering from abusive relationships and intent on creating new, healthier relationships. As with CBT and DBT, patterns are key; identifying them, isolating them, and changing them.

Mentalization-based therapy, or mentalizing, is useful in treating sufferers of BPD. It focuses on understanding their own feelings and thoughts as well as those of other people. Like interpersonal therapy, it's excellent for helping the client to create stronger bonds with others. Victims of abusive relationships and emotional abuse often have troubles integrating with well-adjusted people to form new, healthy relationships.

Psychodynamic therapy focuses on specific experiences which might be formative of unhealthy thought and behavioral patterns, single events as triggers. These can include incidences of abuse, traumatic accidents, sudden family illness or death, or sudden discovery of infidelity, among others. These can easily come into play in emotionally abusive relationships and is frequently used in recovery programs for emotional abuse survivors. It's also commonly used to treat depression, anxiety, and BPD

Emotion-focused therapy (EFT) zeroes in on emotional self-awareness and self-regulation. EFT discourages suppression and encourages plumbing those emotions for their causes. Management techniques are often used, as are visualization and mentalization techniques. As you can imagine, EFT is widely used to treat recovering victims of emotionally abusive relationship. EFT is also often used to treat trauma, social anxiety, depression, eating disorders, relationship and interpersonal issues.

Family therapy focuses on family issues and involves multiple members of the family, depending on the nature of the challenged relationship. Since emotionally abusive relationships are often family oriented, this is a widely used and effective way to treat recoveries from such relationships. It's unfortunate that, in a lot of cases, the relationship had to end, and that's antithetical to a family therapy approach, unless it includes other members of the family. It's also popular for substance abuse and eating disorders, obsessive-compulsive personality disorder, anxiety, and some medical issues.

Group therapy, which lends a support-group quality to psychotherapy, can be extremely effective dealing with emotionally abusive relationships. As these relationships may vary, different perspectives can be extremely valuable. And the consistencies among the abusive relationships means little time or energy is wasted. Just about everybody will have something of value to contribute (and this is just what the victim of emotional abuse needs).

Group therapy has an added advantage which the others lack. They have the perspective of equals. The role of therapist is minimized. This can relieve the stress of being under professional, medical scrutiny. The us-or-them dichotomy of therapist and client is circumvented. There may be less perception of being judged by some elitist. Instead, it's more about being supported.

There could be a flipside to this, and a victimized person may feel ganged-up on in group therapy rather than supported. A well-run group, moderated by a trained and licensed professional, shouldn't give any client real reason to think that, but there could still be that perception just the same. Steps would be taken to prevent or reverse such a misinterpretation, but that's no guarantee that one client or another just won't be comfortable in that kind of setting. Some people may have privacy issues which are unrelated to the group or how it's run. In fact, a room full of clients are not as closely bound to the laws of confidentiality which restricts a therapist's ability to share certain information. Group therapy is simply less confidential by its very nature. Some will be more sensitive to this than others, for a variety of reasons.

Another drawback is that no client will get as much therapeutic time or attention, which they may require. For this reason, group therapy is often recommended as supplemental to concurrent one-on-one psychotherapy.

Group therapy is popularly used to treat childhood and adolescent learning, behavioral, or family issues. It's commonly used to treat interpersonal, medical, aging issues, as well as anxiety, depression, and addictions.

Mindfulness-based therapy focuses on the present. Instead of renumerating about the past (which cannot be changed) or the future (which cannot be controlled), this Eastern-influenced school focuses on the moment. It can bring relief, but is not widely recommended for long-term effects. But it can help with the immediate effects of a breakup, a death, generally most effective when used in conjunction with another therapy for long-term effectuality. Mindfulness-based theory is often recommended for schizophrenia, depression, anxiety, stress, and physical pain. Meditation is a popular and effective adjunct to mindfulness-based therapy.

Creative arts therapy uses methods of creative expression to help the client come to grips with painful, abusive experiences. Dance, poetry, music, and literature are popular in this type of therapy. Since emotionally abusive relationships seek to ensure control over the victim, this therapy finds its effectiveness in giving the client full control. How many of us are free to express ourselves in modern dance or poetry? And these can be surprisingly cathartic and effective in cases of abuse recovery.

In point of fact, much of modern culture is comprised of examples of this practice, but in a non-clinical setting. Bob Dylan gave voice to a generation of newly aware and active youth. He later chronicled his marital woes in songs so stark and personal (on *Blood on the Tracks*) that he recreated what the singer/songwriter could do. Beatle John Lennon put primal scream therapy on single *Cold Turkey*. The Who's Pete Townsend wrote about his childhood abuses in *Tommy*. Silvia Plath chronicled her childhood abuses at the hands of her father, practically launching an entirely new movement in poetry: that of stark, personal confession. The entirety of Britain's punk rock movement was basically a chaotic, united roar against Margaret Thatcher's government, the crass commercialization of the disco era, and just about anything else they could find to object to. Rap and hip hop chronicled urban life in a manner which was also the last great revolution in modern music.

In a clinical setting, creative arts therapy is often used to improve motor function and cognitive skills, encourage emotional stability, treat depression and anxiety, resolve conflicts, and build social skills. Intensive therapy and rapid recovery are the focus.

Inpatient Therapy

Whatever the preferred school, some patients may consider inpatient therapy. It's often considered unnecessary for recovery from most emotionally abusive relationships. For recoveries of this sort, greater independence is often valued, not less. But serious cases may still require inpatient treatment for concurrent conditions, including PTSD, substance abuse, self-harm, and severe, suicidal depression.

We're not here to endorse any particular treatment center, of course. WE don't have any connection to any treatment center, so this isn't sponsored content. But if you're looking at inpatient treatment for PTSD or the other attendant disorders or complexes or conditions and feel inpatient treatment is best, it's a good idea to know what's out there.

In the United States, Bridges to Recovery is a well-known treatment center. Based in Beverly Hills, the facilities offer:

- Six-bed residences with private bedroom
- Alternative to traditional hospital surroundings
- private pool
- Top-quality clinical staff
- Individualized treatment plans
- Healthy gourmet meals
- Yoga
- Meditation

- Acupuncture

Bridges to Recovery specializes in treating:

- Anxiety disorders (OCD, panic disorders, social anxiety)
- Mood (depression, complicated grief, bipolar disorder)
- Various personality disorders (borderline, dependent, and narcissistic personality)
- Various complex psychiatric disorders (schizophrenia)
- Trauma (PTSD, dissociative disorders, childhood trauma)

Favored modalities of psychotherapy include psychodynamic psychotherapy, CBT, DBT, among others.

The Sprout Help Group has facilities on both US coasts and specializes in:

- Comfortable, friendly surroundings
- Focus on continued recovery
- Providing skill sets for life after treatment
- Medical detox as well as inpatient rehabilitation

- Clinical treatment

- Substance abuse withdrawal

- Accountability and support

- Multiple modalities

- Substantial follow-up support after the inpatient course of therapy

Their areas of specialty include treating:

- Addiction

- Psychiatric illness

- Domestic violence

Inpatient care for mental health issues is widely available in the UK too. In some cases, however, the treatment may be involuntary and court-ordered.

The famed Barchester Healthcare facilities can be found all over the UK, including:

- Forest Hospital, in Mansfield: Focuses on specialist requirements such as alcohol-related brain injury, Huntingdon's, early onset dementia.

- Arbour Lodge Independent Hospital, in Marple: Focuses on males 50 years or older with organic or functional diagnoses.

- Jasmine Court Independent Hospital, Waltham Abbey: Treats a wide variety of mental health and behavioral complications.

- Castle Lodge Independent Hospital in Sutton, Hull: Centering on those with varied but more specialized needs, including schizophrenia, bipolar disorder/manic depression, depression, dementia.

- Windermere House Independent Hospital, in Hull: Specializes in chronic or enduring mental illnesses.

- The Billingham Grange Independent Hospital, in Billingham: Serves a wide variety of special needs using a person-centered approach.

Other inpatient healthcare service providers in the UK include Shrewsbury Court Independent Hospital, providing psychiatric rehabilitation for those struggling with aspects of independent living as a result of acute mental and psychological issues, learning debilities, concurrent diagnoses. If offers nursing are, psychological and social services, physical healthcare, occupational therapy, and clinical leadership.

Helplines

Helplines can also be very useful. One can't always just jump right into therapy. Preparations have to be made, financial and logistical. The task of finding treatment, inpatient or otherwise, can be daunting and intimidating, inspiring some would-be patients to forgo treatment altogether. Very real time constraints can be just as daunting as financial or practical limitations. Some things have to be dealt with immediately. For these things, hotlines can be perfect.

Helplines are almost always available at any time of the day or night. They're manned by trained tele-clinicians, often licensed. If you or someone you know find themselves in urgent need of care, consider one of these reliable helplines.

The Suicide Prevention Lifeline is always available and staffed with the best professional crisis counselors. 1-800-273-8255

The National Domestic Violence Hotline is a leading helpline for domestic violence crises. Like the Suicide Prevention Lifeline, this helpline is available around the clock, every day of the week. The National Domestic Violence Hotline offers safety planning and other services which can be life-saving. 1-800-799-7233

The Veterans' Crisis Line is run by the U.S. Department of Veterans Affairs. They specialize in helping traumatized veterans deal with PTSD, anxiety, depression, substance abuse, thoughts of suicide, and can be a bridge to other USDVA services such as finding apartments, jobs, food, and other necessities. Call the at 1-800-273-8255 or text 838255 from a mobile phone.

The Trevor Project is a leading nonprofit which reaches out to, advocates, and provides support to those in the LGBTQ+ community and can help with identity abuses, sexual abuse and discrimination, depression. The line is available around the clock, 365 days a year at 1-866-488-7386.

Along these lines, TransLifeline focuses on gender nonconforming people (transgender, nonbinary). It's open 24/7 to US residents at 1-877-565-8860 and Canadian residents at 1-877-330-6366.

The National Drug Helpline is the ideal go-to for US residents struggling with drug and alcohol addiction. 1-888-633-6239

Less well-known is the US Substance Abuse and Mental Health Services Administration (SAMHSA) Helpline is ideal for concerned love ones, though it's not a crisis counseling service.

Project Safe Place provides shelter and support for children who don't feel safe at home. There are various Safe Place shelters to quickly help sufferers no matter where they are. Just text 69866 for the nearest shelter and to reach a trained professional. The National Runaway Safeline is also available at 1-800-786-2929. The Childhelp National Child Abuse Hotline, available at any hour of the day or night, can be reached at 1-800-422-4453.

The UK provides an exhaustive list of helplines and support groups to, including (but certainly not limited to):

- Samaritans UK & Ireland, for 24-hour emotional support for those at risk of suicide. Twenty branches are open every day of the year. 1 800 116 123
- Connect Counselling offers adults free telephone counselling and support for abuse, trauma, or childhood neglect. 6-10 pm, Wednesday to Sunday. 1 800 477 477 (Ireland), 00800 477 477 77 (UK and Northern Ireland), 00353 (0) 1 865 7495 (Outside ROI and UK)
- Campaign Against Living Miserably (CALM) helps young men between 15-35

deal with suicidal tendencies and depression. 0800 585858

- HopeLine UK offers advice to the suicidal. 0800 068 4141

- Lifeline (N.Ireland) offers support, befriending, mentoring and help treat self-harm, depression, trauma, abuse, and anxiety. 0808 808 8000

- The Premier Lifeline helpline provides support from a Christian perspective. 0300 111 0101

- Breathing Space provides assistance and emotional support in Scotland for depression and suicidal risk. 6 pm to 2 am. 0800 83 85 87

- Scotland's Domestic Abuse and Forced Marriage Helpline, on the other hand, is available all day and night, offering support for survivors of domestic abuse or those trapped in force marriages. 0800 027 1234

- Anxiety UK offers support and information to anxiety condition sufferers in the UK.

Monday to Friday, from 9.30 am to 5.30 pm. 03444 775 774

- Mind offers support and advice to sufferers of mental health problems in the UK. The phone lines are open Monday through Friday from 9 am to 6 pm. 0300 123 3393

- SANE includes families, friends, and careers affected by mental illness. 10 am to 10 pm, Monday – Friday. 0300 304 7000

- Childline offers free, 24-hour confidential and private services to parents and children in the UK. 0800 1111

- Refuge provides 24-hour support and services to UK women and children being victimized by domestic abuse. 0808 2000 247

- National Society for the Prevention of Cruelty to Children (NSPCC) provides 24-hour support and help to UK children being abused or neglected. 0808 800 5000

- Narcotics Anonymous is among the most famous support groups, offering 24/7 help to UK drug addicts.

- Narcotics Anonymous offers support and advice to people in the UK who have a drug problem. The NA Helpline is open seven days a week until midnight. 0300 999 1212

- The Rape Crisis National Helpline provides emotional, confidential support to female victims of sexual violence. Open every day of the year, 12:00 -14:30 and 19:00 - 21:30. 0808 802 9999

Mental Healthcare Apps

If things don't seem that urgent yet, but you're still in the exploratory stages of a therapeutic recovery, consider one of several apps available, each with their own services and specialties.

Some of any healthcare app's natural advantages include accessibility (support, communication, information, available to anyone with a smartphone); anonymity (these apps are private and secure and there's no need to share your name in most cases); convenience (with the variety and ease of use); and engagement (regular notifications and quick, effective interaction with trained professionals at anytime and from virtually anywhere).

Moodfit is perhaps the best mental healthcare app. It specializes in treating anxiety, stress, or depression. *Moodfit* helps the user track their moods to reveal patterns, triggers, and responses, and makes use of CBT. Its pros include:

- Easy adaptability
- Easily customized
- Tracks daily progress
- Actionable exercises
- Visual insights

The app's cons include:

- No access to professional help
- Risk of self-diagnosis
- Some of the advanced features cost more money

- Time-consuming

Another quality mental health app is *MoodMission*, focusing on stress, depression, and anxiety. The app generates exercises, called *missions*, to improve the user's skills or mood. Such missions may include:

- Breathing exercises and other emotion-based practices
- Push-ups and other physical activities
- Learning new skills and other behavioral activities
- Reframing negative thoughts and other thought-based activities

Talkspace is perhaps the best for actual talk therapy. Pros include:

- Access to dialogue with a trained and licensed professional (3,000 hours of training each)
- Wide range of price options
- Various ways of communicating with the therapist
- Professional diagnoses

- Secure and private dialogues

The app's cons include:

- Expensive

- Not for severe mental health issues

- Limited therapeutic range

- Evaluation surveys can be annoying

Sanvello is perhaps most effective for stress relief. It uses clinically validated techniques when dealing with anxiety, stress, and depression. *Sanvello* uses cognitive behavioral therapy to teach mindfulness and track health and mood.

The app's pros include:

- Proven effectiveness

- May be covered by health insurance

- Provides numerous options

- Allows peer-to-peer connection

- Access to a licensed therapist

The app's cons include:

- Not appropriate for severe conditions

- Advanced features require monthly subscriptions

- Expensive premium add-ons

- Lack of clear credentials for the app's *coaches*

- Therapy option may not be available in your state

Headspace is a great meditation app (and there are several of these). Short, daily guided meditation sessions are enjoyed by millions of users in almost 200 countries worldwide.

The app's pros include:

- Options for all skill levels

- Vast information content

- Promotions

- Quick to learn

- Easy-to-use

- Progress tracking

The app's cons include:

- Limited, shorter free options

- Free only up to 10 sessions

- Subscription required

- Discipline required

- Often rudimentary for advanced users

- Not appropriate for severe mental health issues

Happify presents games which are scientifically constructed build resistance, reduce stress, and overcome negativity to change destructive thought patterns. CBT is a significant tool in this app's approach.

The user can pick different tracks to guide the exercises, which then guide the user toward specific goals, such as coping with stress, fueling career success, achieving mindfulness, building self-confidence, and overcoming negative thoughts.

Happify's pros include:

- Activity integration for individualized goals
- Different tracks/goals
- Developed by therapists
- Understanding emotions and moods
- Increased mindfulness

The cons include:

- Some options are premium only
- Limited free version

- Deadlines and challenges can be stressful

The Depression CBT Self-Help Guide educates users about depression and management strategies. It encourages self-care. Some of the app's unique offerings include:

- Depression severity screening test
- Articles about CBT and clinical depression
- A daily thought diary
- Relaxation audio
- Emotion training audio
  The app's pros include:
- Simple instructions
- Easy and effective activities
- Promotes calm
- Symptom severity feedback
- Filled with mental health facts and information
- Free access to activities and content
  The cons of this app include:
- Just for android
- Lack of full CBT data

- Difficult identifying negative emotions and thoughts

- Risk of self-diagnosis

- No professional guidance

Now that should give you everything you need to know about what kind of challenge you're facing and with whom, what the causes might be and what the options are. You'll still have to make your best choices, be flexible in your strategy but inflexible in your resolve, continue to educate yourself and to work through the therapies described in this book.

If you haven't found the right remedy here, perhaps this chapter will lead you to what you're looking for. Please, if you feel we've left anything out, feel free to reach out. We're here for you, and your input may help others as well as us.

CONCLUSION

From the origins of narcissism to the ancient and contemporary history of the family unit, we've seen how these two complex configurations can interact in surprising and destructive ways. What should be the first and primary safe haven becomes a living nightmare, a source of seemingly unending torment which may live on long after the house itself crumbles. The best years of life, what should be the most carefree, become a marathon of misery. Sources of support become twisted fonts of negativity. Childhood cruelties inflict lifetimes worth of damage from which some people never recover. Here we are speaking of the worst crimes a person can commit, in this or in any time. We've looked at some of the worst figures in human history, the manifestation of one disorder we discuss, referred to as *evil incarnate* by one pioneer in the field. But these abuses are far more common than history's greatest villains. In fact, they're often as common and as close as members of our own family.

Worse, these patterns are learned and then taught, handed down from generation to generation. Ignore them now and you know you set others forth on the same pattern, members of a generation you may not know or may never know. And worse than ignoring them, you may have discovered that you were unwittingly enabling them or even emulating them, committing them yourself. You also have the self-awareness and powers of self-regulation to control your own behavior and change your ways of thinking and behaving if this is the case. Only you can do it.

The worldwide statistics have told the tale. Things are worse than they ever have been and they're only likely to get worse. We all owe it to prevent the downward spiral of these learned behaviors, lest we be forced to take responsibility. In this way, if one is not part of the solution then one is likely to be part of the problem. To put it another way, all that is required for evil to prevail is for good people to do nothing.

But that's not you. You know the problem by name, you know it in detail. You know your family, how they may be suffering from these maladies and disorders. Now you know how serious they are, often fatal to those around them.

Now you know how important it is to put these concepts and remedies into effect. You've seen the ramifications of inaction, you know how much is at stake. But you're not about to wait any longer, and why should you? Reading and digesting this book was a great step, but the journey really is just beginning. With this as your roadmap, you're bound to make the journey safely and in good time.

Because you've taken steps to break the cycle of narcissism in your familial relationships. You've learned and observed the subtleties of life in the real world, outside the realm of fairy tales. You've gained a working understanding of some of the most crucial psychoanalytic theories currently at play and even a few cutting-edge notions others aren't likely to know. And you'll know how to share them, with clarity, concision, and empathy, to make everybody's lives better.

You'll know a narcissist when you see one and have the foresight to avoid them if you can, to deal with them when you must, and how to avoid their toxic influence. You'll know where to draw the line and when, even when it comes to your own blood relatives. You know how dangerous, even deadly such relationships can be, how seriously you have to take them. And it doesn't stop at telling you to act, but *how* to act. You now know where to go and when, whom to call. We've done everything but put the phone into your hand.

But we've done more than that. We've given you the preparation, the education, the affirmation. Using what you know here, you can rid narcissism and narcissists, abusive relationships of all sorts from your life, even those who have always been closest to you. And you also have the options for healing, right here at your fingertips. It won't be easy, but you now know what you have to do, how to do it, and when.

Come back to this book often, if you like. Some of it is meant as a reference to be revisited when necessary. Make it a part of your recovery plan toward a better life, a tool you can use and reuse again and again. Then spread your wings to reach new heights. There will always be more to learn, more to know. That's why we're here, with books on every facet of a better, happier, healthier psyche and a more stable, more satisfying, and more successful life.

I hope my own true-life experiences have proven helpful. They are among the most painful experiences of my life. But they were formative, and if they can illuminate your condition or the behavior of others, if they can in any way illuminate the shadows which have encroached upon your lives, then my suffering will be entirely justified and reasonable and, frankly, worth it. Others have been through worse, and I'm grateful to be reminded of that and to have enlightened myself as well. I hope this book brings you as much peace and resolution as it has brought me.

Carry on in good spirits then. Be ready to leave the past behind and give up the future to the fates. The present is yours to control now, and in this you may be handed the keys to the kingdom, a roadmap to the things which have frustrated your search for a better life. Let your frustrations fade and your satisfactions mount, my friends. I'd wish you good luck, but you don't need it. You've already got everything you need. I know you will succeed. We're here for you until that happens, when it happens, and long after.

RESOURCES

https://www.mayoclinic.org/diseases-conditions/narcissistic-personality-disorder/symptoms-causes/syc-20366662
https://www.mayoclinic.org/diseases-conditions/narcissistic-personality-disorder/symptoms-causes/syc-20366662
https://www.webmd.com/mental-health/narcissism-symptoms-signs
https://www.helpguide.org/articles/mental-disorders/narcissistic-personality-disorder.htm
https://www.verywellmind.com/the-history-of-narcissistic-personality-disorder-2795569
https://www.encyclopedia.com/psychology/dictionaries-thesauruses-pictures-and-press-releases/narcissistic-transference
https://en.wikipedia.org/wiki/Self_psychology
https://www.learning-mind.com/famous-narcissists/
https://www.psychologytoday.com/us/blog/communication-success/201908/difference-between-narcissist-vs-narcissistic-behavior
https://www.psychologytoday.com/us/blog/communication-success/201602/10-signs-narcissistic-parent
https://thepsychologist.bps.org.uk/volume-24/edition-3/responding-parent-abuse
https://psychcentral.com/pro/exhausted-woman/2016/12/7-types-of-parental-abuse#1
https://themighty.com/2018/09/abusive-parent-signs/

https://www.ranker.com/list/famous-survivors-of-child-abuse/celebrity-lists

https://www.theguardian.com/film/2008/may/25/biography.film

https://owlcation.com/social-sciences/Ten-Famous-People-Who-Killed-Their-Own-Children

https://www.ranker.com/list/celebrities-charged-with-domestic-abuse/celebrity-lists

https://healthcare.utah.edu/healthfeed/postings/2017/04/celebs-mental.php

https://healthcare.utah.edu/healthfeed/postings/2017/04/celebs-mental.php

https://www.bridgestorecovery.com/blog/a-one-sided-rivalry-the-traumatic-effects-of-narcissistic-personality-disorder-on-siblings/

https://narcissistabusesupport.com/how-to-identify-narcissistic-siblings-narcissistic-brother-sister/

https://www.psychologytoday.com/us/blog/women-autism-spectrum-disorder/202008/5-tips-dealing-narcissistic-siblings

https://dealwithnarcissist.com/narcissistic-siblings-about-signs-of-a-narcissistic-sibling-the-effect-they-have-and-how-to-deal-with-a-narcissistic-sibling/

https://www.nimh.nih.gov/health/topics/attention-deficit-hyperactivity-disorder-adhd/index.shtml

https://www.webmd.com/mental-health/dissociative-identity-disorder-multiple-personality-disorder

https://en.wikipedia.org/wiki/Ptsd

https://queenbeeing.com/step-monster-life-long-effects-narcissistic-step-parent/

https://www.cultivateandflourish.com/should-you-go-no-contact-with-a-narcissistic-step-parent/

https://stepparentmagazine.com/coping-with-narcissistic-stepchildren/

https://thenarcissistinyourlife.com/narcissistic-stepmothers-ultimate-nightmare-for-stepchildren/
https://poemachronicles.com/narcissistic-father/
https://pathwaysfamilycoaching.com/managing-narcissistic-grandparents/
https://www.divorcestrategiesnw.com/2020/06/boundaries-with-narcissistic-grandparents/
https://thenarcissisticlife.com/signs-narcissistic-grandmother/
https://upliftconnect.com/how-to-rebuild-yourself-after-an-emotionally-abusive-relationship/
https://www.psychologytoday.com/us/blog/rediscovering-love/201806/healing-emotional-abuse
https://medium.com/real-life-resilience/how-to-best-recover-from-an-emotionally-abusive-relationship-a896ffbe3d1b
https://www.healthline.com/health/signs-of-mental-abuse#humiliation-negating-and-criticizing
https://www.medicalnewstoday.com/articles/types-of-therapy
https://www.bridgestorecovery.com/post-traumatic-stress-disorder/inpatient-ptsd-treatment-center/
https://www.symptomfind.com/health/10-best-mental-health-hotlines?ad=dirN&qo=serpIndex&o=740013
https://www.sprouthealthgroup.com/resources/inpatient-rehabilitation/
https://www.help4addiction.co.uk/inpatient-rehab-services-near-me-uk/
https://www.carehome.co.uk/mental-health-hospitals/index.cfm/searchcountry/England
https://www.therapyroute.com/article/suicide-hotlines-and-crisis-lines-in-the-united-kingdom

https://www.verywellmind.com/best-mental-health-apps-4692902

https://www.elitedaily.com/dating/how-to-stop-being-codependent-in-relationships/2042683#:~:text=%20How%20To%20Stop%20Being%20Codependent%20In%20Your,Alone%0AAfter%20my%20first%20relationship%20ended%2C%20I...%20More%20